The Impact of the Global Financial Crisis on the Presence of Chinese and Indian Firms in Europe

T0326920

COST – the acronym for European Cooperation in Science and Technology – is the oldest and widest European intergovernmental network for cooperation in research. Established by the Ministerial Conference in November 1971, COST is presently used by the scientific communities of 36 European countries to cooperate in common research projects supported by national funds.

The funds provided by COST – less than 1% of the total value of the projects – support the COST cooperation networks (COST Actions) through which, with EUR 30 million per year, more than 30,000 Europeans scientists are involved in research having a total value which exceeds EUR 2 billion per year. This is the financial worth of the European added value which COST achieves.

A "bottom up approach" (the initiative of launching a COST Action comes from the European scientists themselves), "à la carte participation" (only countries interested in the Action participate), "equality of access" (participation is open also to the scientific communities of countries not belonging to the European Union) and "flexible structure" (easy implementation and light management of the research initiatives) are the main characteristics of COST.

As precursor of advanced multidisciplinary research COST has a very important role for the realisation of the European Research Area (ERA) anticipating and complementing activities of the Framework Programmes, constituting a "bridge" towards the scientific communities of emerging countries, increasing the mobility of researchers across Europe and fostering the establishment of "Networks of Excellence" in many key scientific domains such as: Biomedicine and Molecular Biosciences; Food and Agriculture; Forests, their Products and Services; Materials, Physical and Nanosciences; Chemistry and Molecular Sciences and Technologies; Earth System Science and Environmental Management; Information and Communication Technologies; Transport and Urban Development; Individuals, Societies, Cultures and Health. It covers basic and more applied research and also addresses issues of pre-normative nature or societal importance. The COST website is at http://www.cost.eu

The Impact of the Global Financial Crisis on the Presence of Chinese and Indian Firms in Europe

Françoise Hay, Christian Milelli and Yunnan Shi

sussex
ACADEMIC
PRESS

Brighton • Portland • Toronto

2 4 6 8 10 9 7 5 3 1

First published in 2012 by
SUSSEX ACADEMIC PRESS
PO Box 139, Eastbourne BN24 9BP

and in the United States of America by
SUSSEX ACADEMIC PRESS
920 NE 58th Ave   Suite 300
Portland, Oregon 97213-3786

and in Canada by
SUSSEX ACADEMIC PRESS (CANADA)
90 Arnold Avenue, Thornhill, Ontario L4J 1B5

British Library Cataloguing in Publication Data
A CIP catalogue record for this book is available from the British Library.

Library of Congress Cataloging-in-Publication Data
Hay, Françoise.
The impact of the global financial crisis on the presence of Chinese and
    Indian firms in Europe / Françoise Hay, Christian Milelli and
Yunnan Shi.
p. cm.
Includes bibliographical references and index.
ISBN 978-1-84519-508-3 (p/b : alk. paper)
    1. Corporations, Foreign—Europe. 2. Corporations, Chinese—
Europe. 3. Corporations, East Indian—Europe. 4. Investments,
Chinese—Europe. 5. Investments, East Indian—Europe. 6. Global
Financial Crisis, 2008–2009. I. Milelli, Christian. II. Shi, Yunnan.
III. Title.
    HD2844.H39 2012
    338.8'895104—dc23

2011028428

Typeset and designed by Sussex Academic Press, Brighton & Eastbourne.
Printed by TJ International, Padstow, Cornwall, on acid-free paper.

Contents

Contents

Contents

Foreword

The topic covered in this work is both timely and significant. As outward investment from the non-triad countries continues to increase its share of global outward investment, it is important to understand the extent to which such investment is sustained in the triad host regions and countries and how such investment ventures evolve over time. This is necessary in order to assess the impact of such investment on host societies. Such understanding is also of benefit to home country firms contemplating and planning strategies for overseas investment. Exploring the effects of the global financial crisis on such investment is a crucial element in seeking to estimate future investment flows and their likely impacts.

Françoise Hay, Christian Milelli and Yunnan Shi have done a superb job of describing and assessing the impact of the crisis on such investment flows in the specific case of Chinese and Indian flows into Europe. Drawing on their own regularly updated database, interview data and case studies, they offer a rich and fascinating picture of the differing impacts of the crisis on Chinese and Indian flows into Europe, as well as revealing differences in impact by sector and by host country. They also highlight new trends that are emerging in relation to Chinese and Indian firms investing in Europe since the advent of the crisis.

I congratulate my COST Action colleagues on a particularly valuable contribution. The authors have demonstrated the rich insights that can be attained from a micro focused study of investment flows.

LOUIS BRENNAN

LOUIS BRENNAN is Proposer and Chair, *COST Action IS0905* on 'The Emergence of Southern Multinationals and their Impact on Europe'. He is also Director of the Institute for International Integration Studies, and Associate Professor in the School of Business at Trinity College, Dublin, Ireland.

The Authors

Françoise Hay has a *PhD* in economics (Rennes) and a general interest in Asian economies for both their national development and their integration in the global economy. Over the last few years, her research has focused on the internationalisation of Chinese companies worldwide along with their drivers and strategies in Europe.

Christian Milelli has a *PhD* in economics (Paris). His research interests include growth regime, globalization and FDI with a focus on North-East Asia. Over the last years, his research has focused on the rise of multinational companies originating from China and India. He has various publications in these topics.

Yunnan Shi has a *PhD* in economics (Rennes) and a general interest in the Chinese economy and its foreign economic relations. He has co-edited with F. Hay two research books (in French, Rennes Academic Press): "The rise of power of the Chinese economy" (2005), and "China: forces and weaknesses of an expanding economy" (2006).

Acknowledgements

This publication is supported by COST and it would not have been possible without the inexhaustible support of the Directorate General for Competitiveness, Industry and Services of the French Ministry for the Economy, Finance and Industry. We especially thank Grégoire Postel-Vinay, in charge of the Strategy Unit, Joëlle Le Goff for generously supporting our work, Elisabeth Nullans from the European Policy Coordination Office as well as sector specialists.

We are also grateful to the Ministry for their approval to bring the initial field research to a larger audience.

Aside from this special thanks go to a number of persons who have shared with us their expertise and hospitality:

David Appia, Chairman of *Invest in France*, and his team; Eva Henkel, Public Relations Director and Yi Cao of *Germany Trade & Invest* in Berlin; Martin Pospisil, Director of the Europe Department and his staff in the Czech Ministry of Trade and Industry; Lucie Votavova and Ivana Bradacova of *CzechInvest*, and Bernard Boidin, Economic Counsellor and Head of Economics Department at the French Embassy in Prague and his colleague Cyril Schlund.

We also wish to express our gratitude to all the business leaders in France, Switzerland and the Czech Republic for their welcome and for giving us some of their precious time and insights.

Of course, we alone are accountable for any factual errors or omissions.

List of Boxes, Case Studies, Figures and Tables

Boxes

Cases Studies

Figures

Tables

The Impact of the Global Financial
Crisis on the Presence of Chinese
and Indian Firms in Europe

Chapter 1

Introduction

Chinese and Indian firms are the main investors from emerging economies in Europe, and their presence has expanded since the beginning of the millennium to reach the centre stage (Hay, Milelli and Shi, 2008).

The key issue here is to determine if the global financial crisis of 2008 had noteworthy effects on the European presence of these 'newcomers': those already in place as well as those on the verge of coming.

While any global economic crisis is not neutral for the internationalization process of firms, the current one has significantly impacted the behaviour of investors in general while it further accelerated the shift in global economic power to emerging economies (rapid recovery, booming markets, etc.).

Indeed, this crisis has put a tremendous stress on European economies, whereas it made Asia, Africa or South America more attractive for Chinese and Indian firms because they are new markets and/or endowed with natural resources. In parallel, Chinese and Indian firms have also taken a fresh look at their own fast-growing domestic markets.

As a result, the European zone has become comparatively less attractive. However, these 'newcomers' are always interested in a presence in Europe because they can't get away from it in the frame of their global strategies.

Admittedly, Europe still has undisputable advantages. It has fewer political risks, populations with high disposable income, and it is their leading export market – i.e. the European Union is already the first market worldwide for Chinese consumer goods. In addition, Chinese and Indian firms can tap in Europe quite needed specific assets – e.g. technological expertise, managerial capabilities, brand recognition, marketing skills, sales network – to bolster their development at home and overseas, by buying up low-priced local companies or departments.

The aim of this book is in line with a precursory field research carried out in 2007 by the same authors on behalf of the French Ministry of Economy about the arrival of Chinese and Indian firms in Europe. Due to the deficit of material and the great diversity of firms from both origin, we had no choice but to take up the challenge and set up an *ad hoc* database in order to collect basic information at firm-level.

The book is based on varied empirical materials and opts for a micro economic perspective on FDI as standard macro approach could be misleading and do not provide, in our case, the relevant data and insights. For China, we resorted to a broader view to take into account the sovereign wealth fund and policy banks, such as China Exim Bank and China Development Bank, which increasingly play a role in FDI flows.

Three types of data have been compiled.

The first is a proprietary database, regularly updated, which tracks and collects information related mainly to the creation of new activities or enterprises, and mergers and acquisitions which involve financial equity or buyout of existing enterprises. Besides providing up-to-date and worthwhile information, the dataset allows a comprehensive understanding of the new phenomenon with variations among recipient European countries and industries.

The second type of data is made up of personal interviews, conducted by the authors across Europe. Special attention has been paid to sectors such as car assembly, automotive equipment, telecommunications equipment or renewable energies.

The third type of data consists of specific case studies elaborated by the authors. Far from being anecdotal in the sense that any random new observation may overturn a previous account, case study analysis, carefully selected and conducted as a detailed narrative specific to a given situation, can provide valuable results particularly useful when data are deficient.

The book is structured as follows: After documenting Chinese and Indian FDI outward context for 2008 and 2009 we provide a brief introduction on China and India's international investment position, followed by a focus on mergers and acquisitions carried out by companies from both countries on a global scale to better position their European operations. We then attempt to discern and assess the first impacts of the current global financial crisis on the behaviour of Chinese and Indian companies in Europe using the database, interviews and the case studies.

We maintain the difference introduced when we started the database between mainland Chinese firms and their counterparts from Hong Kong, despite the ever-easier penetration between the two areas since the retrocession (or return) of the City State to Chinese sovereignty in 1997 and other tricky issues. For example, a few investments identified in Europe as coming from Hong Kong have to be re-routed to parent companies located in mainland China, whereas the reverse is also true.

Finally, the book is intended for those who look for basic materials on a very new topic: the arrival in Europe of multinationals from two continental emerging economies. It also provides a first assessment of the impact of the global crisis on their behaviour. Last, it allows us to draw insights and lessons for European countries.

Chapter 2

Chinese and Indian Outward Foreign Direct Investments during the Crisis Years
A micro economic perspective

Table 1 The 10 largest outward FDIs from emerging economies in the world, 2009 (in million dollars)

Country	FDI Stock 2009	FDI Outflow 2009
Hong Kong	834,089	52,269
China	229,600	48,000
Singapore	213,110	5,979
Taiwan	181,008	5,868
Brazil	157,667	−10,084
South Korea	115,620	10,572
India	77,207	14,897
Malaysia	75,618	8,038
South Africa	64,309	1,584
Mexico	53,458	7,596

Source: World Investment Report 2010, UNCTAD.

Hong Kong and China are the first emerging economies in 2009 either in terms of outward FDI stock or outflows (table 1). India is still behind but took the third rank for FDI outflow in 2009. Actually, Asia captured the lion's share in the top league (7 out of 10) with South America in the second place but far behind (2 out of 10).

The Chinese and Indian economies were not spared by the

global financial crisis in 2008 and 2009, despite showing singular resilience and returning swiftly to the path of their previous growth regime.

Box 1   Why a micro economic perspective?

Notwithstanding the difficulty to get data at the firm-level we have persisted in this line because available data, i.e. annual FDI flows and cumulative investment, do not deliver the appropriate outcomes. Indeed, they are definitively hedged by intra-firm investments or simply reinvested earnings. Besides, as they trace only the immediate destinations they may be biased, particularly for Chinese and Indian investments, by several 'circular' flows between China and Hong Kong, for example, with the odd detour via tax havens. In this respect it must be remembered that, according to official statistics for 2008, Hong Kong accounted for 63 per cent of the total FDI position of mainland China, and the Cayman Islands and the Virgin Islands for 17 per cent, whereas mainland China accounted for 44 per cent of the total FDI position of Hong Kong, with the same position for the Virgin Islands.

2.1   The impact of the crisis on the Chinese and Indian economies

We will focus on the main effects of the crisis on the Chinese and Indian economies in relation to the situation of national firms and their investment projects abroad.

2.1.1   In China

Unlike India and most other countries, the effect of the crisis on the Chinese economy has been limited to the real sphere; the financial sphere and the public finances not being affected directly. The main crisis transmission channel has been foreign trade, which was severely depressed by the drop in the demand of its two main consumer goods markets – the European Union and the United States. Overall, Chinese exports fell by nearly 16 per cent in 2009.

The Chinese authorities did not hesitate as the first signs of the crisis popped up in 2008 to put into action a stimulus plan relying mainly on bank credit allocations: priority was given to manufacturing investment which increased by 30 per cent in 2009. The national economy therefore rebounded to reach an 8.7 per cent growth rate for 2009 and even accelerated in 2010. By and large, Chinese companies were not confronted with a credit crunch, even if the situation varies according to the nature of the company, i.e. public enterprises when compared to private ones have a much easier access to financial resources and others (public procurements, for example).

Chinese OFDI flows increased by 132 per cent and 6.5 per cent in 2008 and 2009 respectively, whereas Hong Kong OFDI flows were much more affected in 2008 (–2 per cent) before rising slightly in 2009 (4 per cent).

2.1.2 In India

Despite a banking system fairly well protected against the jolts of globalised finance, the withdrawal of portfolio investments held by foreigners on the Mumbai financial centre resulted in major capital losses: the Sensex composite index lost more than half its value between the beginning and the end of 2008. This pressure, combined with growing economic uncertainties and the rise of interest rates, precipitated an internal liquidity crisis forcing the Indian Central Bank to inject funds to deal with.

The real sphere was similarly affected through foreign trade: exports, the conveyor belt for national manufacturing production, eased back in October 2008 for the first time in fifteen years.

As a result the national economic situation worsened and

prompted the Indian government to resort to Keynesian-type recipes. A first package of measures was taken in December 2008.

Undoubtedly, the global financial crisis was not neutral on Indian firms' investment decisions abroad. OFDI flows which had peaked historically at 17.8 billion dollars in 2007 fell back by 6.3 per cent in 2008, easing further in 2009 (–21 per cent). Such an outcome was not seen since 1999 even though it is in line with the general trend worldwide.

The falling off of Indian investment projects overseas, mainly M&As, concerned the developed countries, particularly the European zone. It was compounded by a credit crunch either in the domestic market or overseas. Indeed, numerous Indian firms, including large diversified groups, were forced to defer national and foreign projects. In addition, those Indian firms which had issued foreign currency convertible bonds to finance their growth strategies encountered unexpected problems, particularly the conversion prospects for these instruments scheduled to mature at the end of 2009 or during 2010. Firms like Subex Azure, Aurbindo Pharma, Orchid Chemicals, Wockhardt, Firstsource or 3i Infotech, which all had an established presence in Europe, find themselves heavily in debt (Pradhan 2009). It is hardly surprising that a company like the drug maker Wockhardt has been forced to sell off all its foreign subsidiaries.

Ultimately, the Indian firms had no real possibilities to get round the financial constraints: neither the opportunity to finance mergers and acquisitions through debt nor to use their assets due to the drop in share values.

2.1.3 The contrasting international investment position of China and India

Overall, countries commit abroad in investment terms not just through FDI but also, and in some cases increasingly, through other types of investment. By expanding the coverage, one can not only compare outward and inward flows and the resulting net positions, but also to discern the emergence of new instruments which may drive FDI flows in the future.

The annual international investment position which deals with assets and liabilities held and released by each country provides an interesting overview: FDI is divided into two main categories, Greenfield and Mergers-and-Acquisitions (M&As), while portfolio investments encompass equity securities, debt securities in the form of bonds, money market instruments, and financial derivatives. Besides portfolio are more volatile in times of crisis. We make use of it for comparing China and India during the 2006–2009 period. By doing so, we take into consideration the pre-crisis and crisis periods (tables 2a and 2b).

The contrasting situation between the two countries is quite clear when viewing the tables side by side.

First, China shows a net positive position with its amount expanding three times between 2006 and 2009, despite significant slowing down over the last two years due to the global financial crisis. At the end of 2009 China

Table 2a Assets and liabilities of China towards the rest of the World, 2006–2009 (in billion dollars)

	2006	2007	2008	2009
Net position	*640*	*1188*	*1 494*	*1 822*
Assets	1 690	2 416	2 957	3 460
Direct Investment Abroad	91	116	186	230
Portfolio investment	265	285	252	243
Other investment (trade credits, loans and deposits)	254	468	552	536
Foreign Exchange Reserves	1 066	1 528	1 946	2 399
Liabilities	1 050	1 228	1 463	1 638
Direct Investment in China	614	704	915	997
Portfolio investment	121	147	168	190
Other investment	315	378	380	451

Source: State Administration of Foreign Exchange (People's Bank of China), 2010.

Table 2b   Assets and liabilities of India towards the rest of the world, 2006–2009 (in billion dollars)

	2006	2007	2008	2009
Net position	*−60*	*−63*	*−50*	*−62*
Assets	184	251	387	341
Direct Investment Abroad	16	31	50	66
Portfolio investment	1.2	0.9	1.5	0.8
Other investment (trade credits, loans and deposits)	15	16	26	25
Foreign Exchange Reserves	145	195	299	238
Liabilities	244	310	437	403
Direct Investment in India	52	78	119	123
Portfolio investment	64	81	118	82
Other investment	127	155	200	197

Source: Reserve Bank of India, 2010.

holds a significant amount of foreign assets in all items, from FDI – 230 billion dollars – to foreign exchange reserves – 2,399 billion dollars which is by far the largest item (70 per cent of total assets). FDI and foreign exchange reserves are the two items which have grown the fastest during the period.[1] In the first case, the dynamics is due to a low starting base, whereas in the second, the performance achieved highlights the central role played by external trade in the Chinese economy. Besides, the effect of the crisis are so far not visible, whereas it is not the same story for port-folio investments abroad, where the amount drops after the peak of end-2007, just before the financial crisis had inten-sified. Lastly, the liability commitment is controlled, with nevertheless a FDI commitment level in China which remains greater than Chinese OFDI, despite foreign investors seemingly moderating or delaying their investment

1 As a matter of fact, foreign exchange reserves reached 2,847 billion dollars at the end of 2010.

projects in China at the end of the period. But this trend will soon resume for two long-lasting reasons: first, the unequivocal will of Chinese authorities to lure foreign investors, in particular those having specific know-how and skills, and second, the attractiveness of a huge and vibrant domestic market as a logical location to invest for foreign companies.

Conversely, India seems overall to be in a less favourable situation. Firstly, it still has a net negative position, this being made worse by the current crisis. Secondly, it only has significant asset amounts for two items – foreign exchange reserves which increased modestly over the period and OFDI which progressed. One can pinpoint the same imbalance as for China to inward FDI.

In sum, China differs from India not only when one compares their international investment position and its components, but also through its ability to mobilise its huge foreign exchange reserves. This capacity was extensively used by the Chinese government during the end of 2010 to provide financial support to several European countries, e.g., Greece, Ireland and Spain, badly affected by the crisis of the sovereign debts.

The general landscape for FDI being in place, we shed light on the mergers and acquisitions conducted by Chinese and Indian firms on a global scale during the 2008–2009 period. Why use this category of investment and not greenfield investments or both? Actually, we resort to mergers-and-acquisitions as a proxy to capture the changing (or not) behaviour of Chinese and Indian companies in Europe in absolute and relative terms?

Several reasons can be put forward:

- The limits inherent to FDI data from balances of payment can be bypassed,
- M&As data are much more rapidly available,
- The time lag in data availability proves very useful during a period of crisis,
- Greater consistency with the database (firm-level),

- Lastly, 'Southern' multinational firms getting more confident used buyouts on a larger extent to rapidly expand their international footing.

2.2 Mergers and Acquisitions made by Chinese firms worldwide during the crisis period

Even if Chinese companies, particularly large State-Owned Enterprises, have so far favoured organic growth, the increase of mergers-and-acquisitions (M&As) initiated by some Chinese firms since the early 2000s has propelled them into the international stage (Hay, Milelli and Shi, 2009). Except in the natural resources field, M&As are generally conducted in a friendly way by targeting troubled firms or even bankrupted ones. The first Chinese overseas acquisitions occurred in mid-1980s, at the same time as foreign companies were entering China as the country opened up. China joined the WTO at the end of 2001, which without question speeded up the fledgling movement. Lenovo's acquisition of the personal computer department of the US giant IBM, in 2004, for 1.2 billion dollars marked a turning point by revealing the capacity of Chinese firms to acquire emblematic companies in industrialised countries.

The boom in Chinese firms making cross-border acquisitions has been rapid and rather unexpected by actors from a country with little experience in the matter. It is true that the acquisitions of foreign firms were given impetus by the government under the title of 'go global' (*zou-chu-qu*, literally 'go out') in the early 2000s. Its aim was threefold: firstly, recycling part of the huge foreign currency reserves, secondly, to ensure the supply safety of natural resources for the national economy, and thirdly, to improve the number and place of Chinese firms taking place in international rankings (*Fortune Global 500*, for example). National pride, prestige and legitimacy for both political and business leaders were clearly at stake (Morck *et al.*, 2008).

Targeted sectors include the exploitation of natural resources, energy sources and 'market finance'. *Ad hoc* instruments have been employed in supporting direct investment abroad – e.g., preferential access to loans, fiscal incentives along with indirect assistance. The regulatory framework for Chinese acquisitions abroad has become more flexible: since August 2008, the approval of the Ministry of Trade is no longer required for acquisitions valued at less than 100 million dollars; instead they fall under the sole responsibility of provincial or municipal authorities which, on principle, give favourable approval.

The purpose of this section is to explore the impact of the global financial crisis on the acquisition of overseas firms by Chinese companies.

It is important to remember, straight away, that one effect of the crisis has been to slow down cross-border M&As worldwide in both number – 50 per cent drop between 2007 and 2009 – and in value – 32 per cent downturn in the total amount of transactions between 2008 and 2009, and 53 per cent between 2007 and 2009.

Chinese cross-borders M&As have followed the same path. Having gained 44 per cent in value in 2008 over 2007, to reach 73 billion dollars, Chinese acquisitions fell by 27 per cent the following year (43 billion). Nonetheless, Chinese M&As have fallen less than those of the rest of the world, with even greater amounts invested than in previous years. The result is growth in the relative share of China in the total number of cross-border M&As worldwide, with a previously unknown level of 7.5 per cent achieved in 2009 after an average of 2 per cent throughout the previous ten years. Therefore, for the last period China ranked third just behind the United States and France.

Chinese firms have made 705 overseas M&As (excluding transactions both ways between mainland and Hong Kong firms): 335 are by mainland firms and 370 by Hong Kong firms. One thing is confirmed: Hong Kong firms are far more internationalised, relatively speaking, than their mainland counterparts: 15 per cent of their M&As are made on the international market against 6.6 per cent for firms from mainland China. Such a result was expected given their history and also the respective size of the home country.

We then looked at the main features of these transactions: geographical patterns, sectoral distribution and commitment levels of investors, i.e. main firms investing abroad, shareholding votes and amounts invested.

2.2.1 *Geographical pattern of Chinese M&As*

Ten countries account for more than 70 per cent of all Chinese overseas M&As for the 2008–2009 period. Australia (18.6 per cent) and the United States (11.2 per cent) head the league by some margin. Then come Canada (8.2 per cent), Singapore (7.5 per cent), Virgin Islands (6.2 per cent), United Kingdom (4.7 per cent), Japan (4.4 per cent), Taiwan (3.8 per cent), Indonesia (2.8 per cent) and India (2.7 per cent).

Both mainland and Hong Kong firms favour the same countries, albeit in a slightly different order of preference: although Australia is well ahead in both cases, the United States and Canada come next for mainland firms, and Singapore and the Virgin Islands for Hong Kong firms.

Asia is the largest target area, with 30 per cent of the Chinese M&As abroad for the 2008–2009 period. Geographical and cultural proximity explain this outcome along with strategic motivations. Three countries – Singapore, Japan and Taiwan – account for over half these acquisitions. Singapore is in the first place mainly due to the preferential cultural, ethnic (diaspora) and financial relationships between the two City States of Hong Kong and Singapore.

Japan comes next. This is a rather unexpected outcome given the high entry barriers and the technological-intensive level achieved by the Japanese industry. Actually, it stems from the recent Japanese opening up to inward FDI and M&As to foreign firms, as well as a fallout from numerous partnerships forged by Japanese firms in China with firms which are now trying to scale up their activity. One can see a marked interest in technology-intensive activities/sectors such as software development or electrical-electronic equipment.

Taiwan lies third with mainland and Hong Kong firms showing equal preference for financial and computer sectors.

The second place held by Oceania, essentially Australia, in the Chinese acquisitions is quite surprising. Actually, it is driven by a buyout spree of mining deposits in over three quarters of cases.

Then comes North America. This geographical area became the leading destination for mainland firms with nearly a quarter of their overseas acquisitions made there for the reference period. It reflects the substantial financial and trade links between the two countries before the crisis, added to which are acquisition opportunities, given the severity of the financial crisis. These acquisitions are fairly diversified with strong points in new technologies, equipment, leisure industry, natural resources and even in 'market finance', despite the huge losses occurred by Chinese investors in US financial institutions.[2]

Europe comes in fourth with the United Kingdom being the focus of more than one-third of acquisitions. It is followed, especially for mainland firms, by Italy and Germany, the Netherlands and France. If the number of M&As are relatively limited in Europe when compared to other areas, they are however strategic from an European point of view. Furthermore they have to be accompanied by numerous greenfield investments made across Europe, particularly in representatives and sales offices.

South America and Africa bring up the rear, where Chinese and Indian investors have a clear preference for greenfield-type transactions, sometimes barter transactions for Chinese investors: delivery of raw materials against financing lines

2 In 2008, the Chinese sovereign wealth fund lost nearly 1.5 billion dollars in the value of its equity participation in the US private equity fund Blackstone. Its misfortune was similar to another equity participation in the US investment bank, Morgan Stanley (minus 30 per cent).

under linked bilateral aid, with construction of infrastructures or public buildings. The reason given is that there are few businesses for sale (or for purchase) in either of these areas.

2.2.2 Sectoral distribution of Chinese M&As

Chinese cross-border mergers and acquisitions cover a wide spectrum of activities.

The exploitation of natural resources, energy sources and agriculture have attracted Chinese firms, which have become the leading investors in these sectors worldwide in recent years, and account for 40 per cent of Chinese overseas acquisitions. Investments in mines and petroleum cover 27.5 per cent of Chinese M&As with huge geographical concentration (46 per cent in Australia and 22 per cent in Canada). There are two main concurring reasons for the importance of this sector. Firstly, there are the weakened multinational mining groups, sometimes at the end of their tether, which are facing major cash flow problems due to balance sheets weighed down by serving debts contracted before the financial crisis, by frenzied growth strategies based on highly-optimistic forecasts. Secondly, there are the large Chinese State-Owned Enterprises which have access to vast financial resources. They expand their international presence and also follow the desire of senior Chinese leaders to secure the country's supplies of natural resources and energy to sustain a high economic growth.

Finance and real property, with 16.2 per cent of the total, are the second largest sector for Chinese mergers and acquisitions abroad. The Virgin Islands are the destination or transit point of a quarter of finance-related M&As, many of which come from Hong Kong. These transactions are clearly guided by a purely financial logic and include a certain number of manipulations. The services sector is third (15 per cent) with IT in pole position. These activities correspond to the emergence of new sectors in China and mainly take place in Singapore, the United States, South Korea and Japan.

The equipment sector in the broadest sense comes next (11.7 per cent). Electrical and electronic equipment is the leading item, with nearly 60 per cent of acquisitions made in this sector. Three countries stand out: the United States (20 per cent), Italy and Japan (9 per cent each).

Note also the new significance of 'green' activities (4.2 per cent) beyond the sectors listed above, which account for over 80 per cent of Chinese M&As abroad for the 2008–2009 period.

2.2.3 Commitment levels

Most Chinese firms involved in M&As abroad in the 2008–2009 period only made one transaction. However, some companies made several investments in different zones. By way of illustration, we can spell out some investors having made four or more transactions such as:

• Hunan Nonferrous Metals (mining sector; Australia and Canada),
• Sun Hung Kai Invest (mining sector; three of them in Australia),
• Sinochem (petroleum; Australia, India and the United Kingdom),
• Suntech Power (renewable energies; Germany, United States and Russia),
• Industrial and Commercial Bank of China (banking sector; Canada, Russia, Taiwan and Thailand).

JNMC Jinchuan (cobalt, nickel, platinum, etc.; Australia, Canada and Kenya) stands out for 6 transactions and CDC Software for 7. The latter bought out several software publishers and computer service businesses (United States, Canada and United Kingdom), with the stated intention of expanding its offer and achieving bottom-line objectives. It failed, however, in its hostile bid to takeover Chordiant Software (USA).

Chinese firms normally tend to keep their overseas business acquisitions under wraps, all the more so that the severity of the current crisis is likely to stir up nationalism and emphasise xenophobic feelings. In addition, 'bargain hunters' are showing a growing interest in small and medium-sized companies requiring modest investments at the same time as an increasing preference for minority equity investments.

M&As made abroad by Chinese firms in the 2008–2009 period are majority holdings in 58 per cent of cases, and nearly 70 per cent of M&As involve amounts lower than 50 million dollars. Note that the most modest are the most numerous, whilst nearly half are valued at less than 10 million dollars. Having said that, the proportion of investments higher than 100 million dollars is fairly large and basically covers the natural resources-energy sector for acquisitions made in Australia and Canada. For example, Yanzhou Coal Mining paid out 2.8 billion dollars to acquire the Australian company Felix Resources whilst Petrochina spent 1.7 billion dollars on acquiring 60 per cent of the Canadian company Athabasca Oil.

2.3   Mergers and Acquisitions by Indian firms worldwide during the crisis period

Like their Chinese counterparts, Indian firms have been scaling up their M&A activity abroad since the early 2000s. Nonetheless, the Indian firms started the process earlier than mainland Chinese firms. Some Indian firms acquired well-known and symbolic companies in industrialised countries during the 2000s. Transactions abroad once more represent only a tiny part of M&As carried out by Indian firms, with the lion's share being made inside India.

We have extracted from the Thomson Reuters database 375 equity investment or M&As initiated by Indian firms abroad for the 2008–2009 period, slightly higher than similar transactions made by mainland Chinese firms.

2.3.1   Geographical pattern of Indian M&As

Europe comes first with 34.5 per cent of transactions, followed by North America (24 per cent) and Asia (19 per cent). Then come Africa (8 per cent), Oceania (7 per cent) and South America (4 per cent). Although there is no surprise in finding the developed countries (Europe first) as the leader, the position of Africa and South America is surprising. However, this in no way means that Indian investors are disinterested in these geographical areas. The significant proportion held by Oceania (actually Australia with the exception of one trans-action in New Zealand), which is basically motivated by the access to natural resources, leads us by extension to remember that Indian firms have carried out greenfield investment in the natural resources sector in Africa and, to a lesser extent, in South America. They therefore fall outside the radar screen retained here. Nonetheless, the limited number of Indian acquisitions can be explained by the small number of local firms for sale in Africa and by specific conditions in South America.

A more detailed analysis reveals the following order of priority for all host countries: the United States (21 per cent) is well in front of the United Kingdom (10 per cent), which is the leading European country for this mode of investment. Converging factors can explain this order, i.e. historical, cultural and linguistic links and the importance of business services within the UK economy. Then come Australia and Germany (6 per cent respectively) before Italy and Indonesia (5 per cent respectively). Indonesia is the leading Asian destination country, partly because of its geographical proximity and the not-to-be-missed opportuni-ties in the natural resources sector. France is just behind along with Singapore and South Africa (4 per cent respec-tively). South Africa is the prime destination on the African continent due to its development level, opportunities in the natural resources sector and the presence of a large Indian community acting as a go-between for the reception and installation of any new Indian investor in South Africa and neighbouring countries.

2.3.2 Sectoral distribution of Indian M&As

A look at the sectoral distribution for Indian mergers and acquisitions outside their country of origin mirrors both the competitive advantage and/or the primacy of external growth strategies of specific sectors such as pharmaceuticals.

The professional services sector (20 per cent) comes first, followed by natural resources (14 per cent), including a major share held by mining (11 per cent). The pharmaceutical industry (8 per cent) comes next, followed by industrial machinery (6 per cent); car manufacture, software and chemicals are at parity (5 per cent) and telecommunications (4 per cent) bring up the rear. This pecking order is in line with the recognised competitive advantages of Indian firms, with two reservations. Firstly, the place reserved for international acquisitions in the natural resources sector, reminiscent of frenzied acquisitions by Chinese firms, is explained by India also seeking raw material and fossil energy supply safety in an international context of shortages and geopolitical tensions. Secondly, the relatively few acquisitions in software and IT-enabled services, which is recognised as the strong point of national industry, are explained first and foremost by the predominance of organic growth strategies in this sector. Indeed, the business model underlying the success of this sector is based on integrating numerous sales offices and service delivering overseas, and Indian sites responsible for the development and remote maintenance (including back office operations). Local presence is essential in order to be close to customers so as to be able to give better service and also increase their market shares, especially in continental Europe when compared to the United States (Hay, Milelli and Shi, 2008).

The comparison between destination sectors and areas reveals a greater sectoral diversity in Europe than in North

America. The main concentration is found in professional services, with almost double the share of Europe (54 per cent against 24 per cent in the United States), pharmaceuticals where Europe is slightly ahead of North America (37 per cent against 33 per cent) and software which against all expectations sees Europe overtaking North America (47 per cent against 37 per cent). This last observation is explained by the willingness of Indian firms to corner larger market shares in Europe, thereby counterbalancing their huge exposure to the North American market revealed by the crisis.

Apart from the previous sectors, Europe leads in car manufacture and in electrical and electronic equipment. Europe is unquestionably the preferred worldwide location for Indian cross-borders M&As in car manufacture. The proof lies in the many local acquisitions to obtain world-renowned brands (Jaguar and Land Rover acquired by Tata Motors, for example) or numerous car parts manufacturers with specific expertise or *niche* markets and which have close relations with the major European or foreign assemblers established in Europe. Lastly, Asia is well represented in the mining sector (50 per cent).

2.3.3 Commitment levels

Nearly 250 Indian firms were involved in overseas M&As in the 2008–2009 period. If most investors were involved in a single transaction, several groups carried out some transactions in different geographical areas. These include the Reliance Group with 15 acquisitions, the Tata Group with 10 transactions, the Essar Group and Lupin Group equal with 7, and GMR Infrastructure and Mahindra & Mahindra with 6 each. A variety of activity sectors are involved.

Lastly, given the low shareholding levels available (56 per cent) no attempt has been made to breakdown the actual type of control. This is even truer for the amounts with only 33 per cent of transactions recorded for this variable. Having said that, based on available shareholding levels, it is clear that the average commitment is 80 per cent and the median 100 per cent: in short, the Indian firms listed were seeking outright control.

The amounts invested cover a large spectrum: from less than one million dollars to more than 2.3 billion dollars. The average of available expenditure is 80 million dollars whereas the median is at 21 million dollars.

Chapter 3

European Investments by Chinese and Indian Firms in the Financial Crisis

This section is based on investment operations carried out by Chinese and Indian firms. The data used comes from several sources: the Thomson Reuters database for equity investments or mergers and acquisitions, the European Investment Promotion Agencies, especially the 'Invest in France Agency' for new investments, and French and foreign press and specialized magazines.

The data relate to Chinese or Indian groups from industry and services which have invested in Europe, excluding family and individual businesses – e.g. restaurants, small retail businesses, independent import and export offices. The resulting subsidiaries are mainly dedicated to sales or manufacturing activities, with R&D and regional coordination (European headquarters) functions taking off. Apart from the standard threshold of 10 per cent for equity participation we put a cut-off at 10 employees. The scope coverage includes greenfield investments, extensions, equity participations, M&As, joint ventures and closures.

The dataset includes 504 Chinese groups (304 from mainland China and 199 from Hong Kong) and 420 Indian groups for the period of reference.

Although the approach applied here allows for a better grasp of the behaviour of foreign investors through their affiliates, in contrast to FDI data from balance of payments, it does not resolve all the problems. For instance, it would make economic sense to enlarge the database coverage to Chinese or Indian acquisitions of local firms in the United States which have an established presence (affiliates) in Europe.[3]

In order to obtain greater insight we resorted to case studies. By focusing on specific cases beyond the usual ones (Haier and Lenovo for Chinese firms, or Tata for Indian firms) we provided a very useful supplement to the descriptive statistics drawn from the dataset. In addition, as there is no 'representative' or 'typical' firm in both sub-categories we had to resort to numerous case studies.

The financial crisis which has altered the world setting has highlighted the weaknesses of industrialised countries whilst accelerating the rising tide of emerging economies, led by China and India. But what about their firms and their related international engagements? By calling into question their very nature and their purpose we took up the challenge to investigate the behaviour of Chinese and Indian investments in Europe since the onset of the crisis. Have they slowed down or surged forward? Have the main features that stood out in the previous period changed in any way? If yes, then how? Have these investors ultimately responded in similar fashion?

3.1   A contrasting situation between the two categories of investors

The new millennium heralded a rise in Chinese and Indian investments in Europe. They constitute a new wave of investments from Asia, following on from the Japanese wave in the 1980s and a lesser South Korean wave in the 1990s.

Many analysts wondered if this trend was sustainable, whereas others feared being stripped of technology and

3 By acquiring the North American Novelis Group, world leader in aluminium rolling, at the end of 2008, the Indian firm Hindalco (Birla Group) took control of a French factory in Rugles (Eure) with 400 employees. This transaction was barely noticed in France, unlike the Mittal takeover of Arcelor in 2006.

know-how even if the amounts in play were, and indeed still are, limited, or being under risk of an 'invasion'. In the case of China, people felt growingly uneasy by such State-driven form economic relations, since it is actually still a Communist party-State (Yeung and Liu, 2008).

However, this trend became every year more intense until 2007. These new investors, including those from mainland China, are now perceived and considered as similar to other foreign investors, and are welcomed in Europe, particularly greenfield investments. Note that Chinese firms in particular have given new life to several distressed European companies through outright acquisitions or equity participations. Besides, they are courted by European Investment Promotion Agencies in their home country through the set up of representative offices.

The initial results drawn from the dataset and personal interviews clearly show a contrasting situation between the two categories of investors. On the one hand, Chinese investments in Europe have continued to forge ahead, with even an upsurge for mainland China investments, and on the other hand, Indian investments have contracted, in line with the majority of worldwide investors. They reflect the collapse of equity prices and a more stringent access to credit markets as well as rising uncertainty over economic prospects. Conversely, the behaviour of Chinese firms is quite atypical and relates to the unique domestic political-economy context.

3.1.1   The Chinese investments which have intensified in Europe despite the crisis

Investments made by Chinese firms in Europe have continued to increase over the last two years following a downturn in 2006 (figure 1). The drop in 2006 is partly explained by the

4 TCL was the first Chinese firm whose investments failed at a large scale in Europe. Between 2002 and 2006 the firm bought out prestigious European firms such as Schneider Electronics in Germany, and Thomson

Figure 1   Chinese and Hong Kong investments in Europe, 2002–2009 (vertical axis = number of transactions)

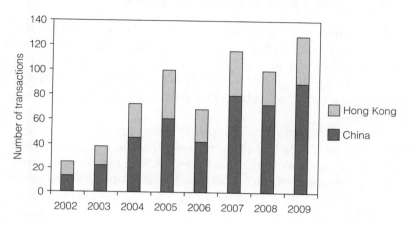

Source: Authors' database.

'TCL syndrome'[4] and the need of a pause after a period of buoyant investments, especially since 2002. Indeed, mainland China investment projects since 2002 have made visible progress both in terms of absolute value and compared with Hong Kong projects. The number of Chinese investments in Europe was split fifty–fifty between mainland China and Hong Kong firms in 2002, but seven years later the split had become 3/4 to 1/4 in favour of mainland China. This is not just due to the crisis, as it was already visible in 2006.

Although the number of Chinese investments in Europe has continued to rise in 2008 and 2009, less headway has nevertheless been made than in the rest of the world, especially in the geographical areas and countries possessing mineral, energy or agricultural raw materials.

———

TV and Alcatel Mobile in France. But all these acquisitions were stinging defeats and inclined the other Chinese investors to be more cautious afterwards.

3.1.2 But the Chinese firms are already more cautious when making their investment decisions

The Chinese investment projects initiated during the economic crisis are, as expected, better prepared, with clearer geographical and sectoral targets. These investors also keep out of the public view, to avoid fuelling protectionist reflexes or even xenophobic feelings in a Europe plunging deeper into the crisis.

Remember that most Chinese investors are looking at long-term strategies. When they invest in Europe it is not to earn money at any price in the first years, but first to gain a foothold in the European markets, particularly in wholesale and retail trade, because the Chinese economy is still an export-driven economy with the European zone already its first foreign market; and second, to get specific assets – e.g. such as technology, skills or established brands – to expand at home and overseas. In addition, as they are largely backed by their state their investments are easier to finance and less risky: as a result, they can accept low-return in their operations contrary, for example, to the Indian groups which are basically private entities.

The French manager of a Chinese firm surveyed made a revealing point. Most Chinese firms do not have an expansionist spirit *per se*, they simply wish their European acquisitions to serve their parent companies and Chinese subsidiaries. This coincides with the observation made by some analysts on the so-called 'light touch' approach following the acquisition of foreign firms by Asian firms, mainly Chinese: corporate stability takes precedence over everything else (Cogman and Tan, 2010).

However, Chinese investors have also taken into account the new opportunities arising from the financial crisis. The emphasis put on new sectors to invest, such as equipment for renewable energy (solar panels, for instance), provides some empirical evidence.

3.1.3 The Indian investments which are contracting

After a peak reached in 2006–2007, the number of Indian investment transactions has dropped off sharply during the crisis (figure 2). There was some decline in 2008 but the following year saw a sharp downturn in the number of transactions, to the point of dropping below the 2005 level and only achieving half the peak of the following year.

This contrasting trend between Indian and Chinese investments in Europe is no doubt related to the fact that the Indians invest most frequently in IT-enabled services and financial services, which have been more affected by the financial crisis.

Figure 2   Changes in Indian investments in Europe, 2002–2009 (vertical axis = number of transactions)

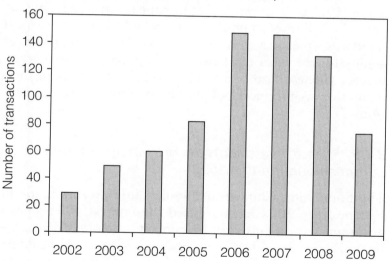

Source: Authors' database.

3.1.4   Europe remains attractive for both investors

Europe still holds several advantages for Chinese and Indian investors. It is a highly-integrated geographical area in terms of institutions (European Union), economy (single market), currency (Euro zone) and movement of people (Schengen area). In addition, Europe has a population of 500 million of high-income consumers, an area of outstanding political stability, an efficient transport infrastructure network, all this with a qualified labour force and first-class technologies and skills, that is specifically researched by investors from emerging economies which are embarked on an unabated catching-up move.

It is therefore hardly surprising that Europe is still a market not to be ignored, despite the current crisis. But, as indicated previously for Chinese firms, any foreign firm intending to set up in Europe or acquire a local firm has stepped further back than during previous years. The effects of the crisis are combined here with the lessons learned from unfortunate experiences faced by firms of the same nationality.

For Chinese investors, a European presence means obtaining a European production label which, given the local standards – the most stringent in the world – is a guarantee of quality for the other markets, including the Chinese market. Indeed, Chinese firms really need to rid themselves of their reputation as producers of shoddy quality goods (see case study 5).

3.1.5   These investments are growingly targeted by European public authorities

The flourishing Chinese and Indian investments made in Europe since 2002 have aroused the interest of European governments and European Investment promotion agencies – be national, regional or even local – to attract and facilitate more investments. This is well illustrated by the set up of numerous branch offices, such as in Mumbai, the economic capital of India, in Bangalore and Hyderabad, the Indian Mecca for new technologies, or in Beijing, the political capital of China, in Shanghai, the economic capital, or in other Chinese economic centres like Guangzhou in the South or Chongqing in the Centre.

At the same time, questions are arising over the sale of European firms or departments to Chinese or Indian investors likely to end up competing with our products. The issues at stake are not negligible. For Chinese firms, the profitability of European subsidiaries seems to be frequently subjugated to the growth of their market shares; the competition conditions are therefore likely to be sidestepped.

But European firms are also looking for a Chinese presence, and a reciprocity somehow would be welcome. For instance, equity investments made in European companies by Chinese firms could greatly enhance the success of the European partner on the huge Chinese domestic market. Further, the CEO of a German company recently underlined the advantage of letting Chinese investors set up a presence in Germany as follows: *China is where German companies are building the most factories. No other market carries so much hope. When you are pleased to have Chinese buyers, you have no right to turn investors away.* Furthermore, the minority equity investment of Fosun in Club Med in June 2010 as part of its expansion into China illustrates the mutual advantages of the opening up.

Lastly, given the increasing number of partnerships between European firms and Chinese groups, especially for technology transfer, one has to wonder over the on-going difference between a transfer taking place on Chinese soil – which is normally approved and encouraged because the European firm is setting up in China – and in Europe as an acquisition or a majority Chinese joint venture – which is usually criticised. In both cases, the technology is pooled and absorbed by the Chinese partner and therefore slips out of the hands of its owner/designer.

3.2 The main characteristics of Chinese and Indian investments made during the crisis in Europe

To be sure, the crisis had a real impact on the characteristics of Chinese and Indian investments corresponding to the pre-crisis period, from 2000 to 2006. We will list and document the main changes. However, as said previously it is too early to have a definitive idea of the nature of such changes.

3.2.1 Lower amounts

Investments made in 2008–2009 involved lower amounts than before the crisis due to strained access to financial resources. The outcome was: greenfield investments of minor size, acquisitions of companies or/departments with values depreciated by the financial crisis, or a desire to avoid acquiring large or emblematic European firms likely to stir economic nationalism.

The amounts of Chinese investments are not all known. Based on a sample of 145 transactions for 2008–2009, where the amounts are known, less than 10 million dollars were committed in 42 per cent of cases and less than 50 million dollars in three-quarters of cases.

The information rate for Indian firms is even less (1/20), nevertheless there is a concentration of data available indicating around 30 million dollars.

3.2.2 The rise in equity investments and M&As

The gap persists between a Chinese profile where greenfield investments dominate (52 per cent of total cases) and a Hong Kong and an Indian profile where equity investments and M&As are the majority (60 per cent and 52 per cent respectively) (table 3). The fall of Indian investments in last years have affected greenfield investments in Europe even more than other modes of entry, which nevertheless have seen a

Table 3 Modes of entry of Chinese and Indian firms in Europe, 2008–2009 (in number)

Modes/Origins	Mainland China	Hong Kong	India
Greenfield Investments	97	21	83
Equity investments and M&As	65	42	107
Extensions	18	6	14
Joint ventures	6	1	3

Source: Authors' database.

reduction in their average unit worth, as mentioned above.

Chinese acquisitions have nonetheless increased over the period to reach 43 per cent of cases, which conveys the mobilisation of substantial financial resources and a firm support from central State or provincial governments. This frequently involves transactions by former sub-contractors, suppliers or partners of European firms in joint ventures or other arrangements. As a result, internal workings, know-how and the manufacturing lines hold no more secrets for them. They can provide liquidity and take over their debt, but the challenge is not negligible as it often entails companies which seasoned Western managers have been unable to turn round. These buyouts normally keep the activity in place with, in some cases, a duplication activity in China, or a relocation of all the firm's manufacturing lines combined with sales offices or outlets maintained in Europe.

The extension projects start to be visible for both categories of investors, with the same share (7 per cent) for Chinese and Indian firms. In some ways, this is a sign that these new investors are well integrating within European economies and local communities. The trend mainly covers the equipment sector (mechanical engineering and electrical equipment) for Chinese firms and IT services for Indian firms.

However, joint ventures with about three per cent respectively of the total of both Chinese and Indian investment projects are not a valued entry mode for these investors into

Table 4 Main European destinations for Chinese and Indian investments, 2008–2009 (in number)

Host countries/ Home countries	China	Hong Kong	India
United Kingdom	42	23	88
France	34	12	26
Germany	31	9	32
Italy	18	3	17
Spain	9	6	6
Netherlands	8	6	6
Switzerland	7	3	4
Central Europe	20	2	17
Scandinavia	4	2	7
Other	9	3	4

Source: Authors' database.

Europe. This confirms their desire to assert their full autonomy along the value chain as Chinese firms have done for the textile and the clothing sectors.

3.2.3 United Kingdom, France and Germany remain the leading destinations in Europe

The market size premium has been maintained and even strengthened during the crisis: the United Kingdom, France and Germany are the destination of 60 per cent of Chinese investments toward Europe since 2008, and 70 per cent of Indian investments for the same period (table 4). Note the increased appeal of the United Kingdom for both investor categories even it is more eye-catching for Indian investments (figures 3 and 4): 43 per cent of the total for 2008–2009. India therefore overtook France in 2009 as the second largest foreign country investing in the United Kingdom behind the United States.[5]

5 According to the British Ministry of Trade and Industry.

Figure 3   Main host European countries for Chinese investment – before 2002, 2002–2007 and 2008–2009

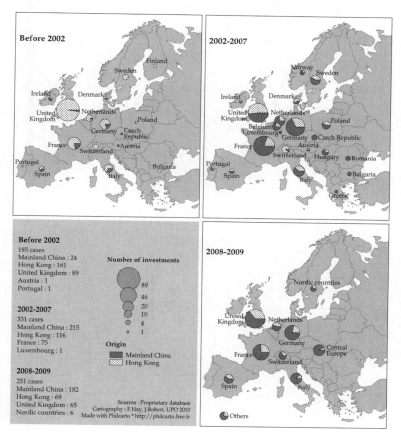

The United Kingdom appeals similarly to mainland Chinese firms: it even becomes their first destination over the period 2008–2009 while it ranked third over the period 2002–2007.

The leading European threesome is followed by Italy, Spain, the Netherlands and Central European countries. It must be remembered that a marked interest by Chinese and Indian investors in Central European countries during the 2007 surveys has not apparently been able to withstand the crisis:

Figure 4 Main host European countries for Indian investment – before 2002, 2002–2007 and 2008–2009

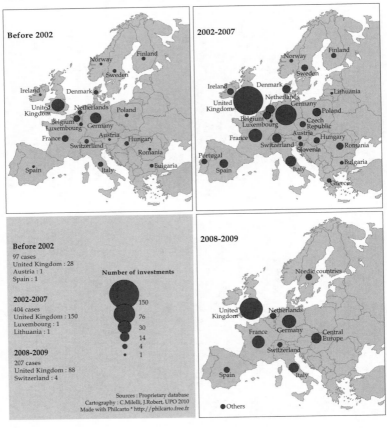

decisions made before the crisis to invest in Central Europe have seen the lowest rate of effective achievement when compared to other European countries (par. 2.3.6). The main Central European destinations are: Poland with 8 Chinese projects and five Indian for 2008–2009, Romania (5 Chinese projects and 5 Indian), and the Czech Republic (6 Indian projects and 2 Chinese).

3.2.4   A contrasting sectoral distribution

If the financial crisis may well have little effect on the sectoral distribution of Indian investment in Europe, it seems on the reverse to have some impact on the array of Chinese sectors already present in Europe: emergence of new sectors along with minor modifications to the distribution pecking order.

Chinese investments

The number of sectors covered by Chinese investors has without doubt increased during the crisis. Admittedly, equipment still occupies a central place in the investment flows from mainland China (table 5a). This sector is driven by car manufacture, with one-third of investments going into the United Kingdom, electrical-electronic equipment (mainly into France, Italy and Spain) and mechanical engineering (Germany, France and Italy).

Chinese investments in information technologies and telecommunications (ITC) are now significant. This is a new trend, since these activities were previously an Indian privilege. This is due to new investments in software and related services by mainland firms, with nearly half focusing on the United Kingdom (figure 3). Firms such as eBaoTech (see case study 3), Neusoft and Bleum are particularly active in this sector.

There is still substantial investment in the telecommunications sector, with Germany receiving nearly one-third. Consider, for instance, Huawei Technologies who moved its European headquarters from London to Düsseldorf along with the set up of R&D facilities.

Investments in renewable energies virtually exclusively from mainland China, which were practically non-existent before the crisis, have accounted for a significant proportion since 2008 (about 11 per cent of investments in Europe). The importance of these investments must however be tempered by the fact they relate mainly to sales activities. They have been stimulated by the effects of the crisis in both China and

Table 5a Sectoral distribution of Chinese and Hong Kong investments, 2008–2009 versus 2000–2007 (in number)[6]

Sectors/Home countries/ Periods	China	Hong Kong	2008–2009
Equipment, including:	49	8	57
Electrical-Electronic	*15*	*3*	*18*
Mechanical engineering	*15*	*1*	*16*
Car manufacture	*16*	*3*	*19*
Other	*3*	*1*	*4*
ITC, including:	31	8	39
Software	*16*	*5*	*21*
Telecommunications	*15*	*3*	*18*
Energy, including:	28	2	30
Renewable	*26*	*1*	*27*
Other	*2*	*1*	*3*
Textile-Clothing	13	13	26
Bank-Finance	14	3	17
Transport-Logistics	5	12	17
BioChemicals-Pharmaceuticals	11	1	12
Metals and Materials	13	2	15
Hotels and Real Property	2	7	9

Source: Authors' database.

the rest of the world. Germany has received 41 per cent of these new investments and France 22 per cent. Suntech Power and Yingli Green are the most active investors and some Chinese companies are even considering setting up assembly units in Europe.

6 For information, we indicate the relative shares of the concerned Chinese activities before and since 2008 : Equipment 34.2% → 22.6%, ITC 13.9% → 15.5% (among it software 2.3% → 8.3%), Energy 2.7% → 11.9% (among it renewable 1.4%à10.7%), Textile-Clothing 11.1% → 10.3%, Bank-Finance 3.4% → 6.7%, Transport-Logistics 25.3% → 6.7%, Biochemicals-Pharmaceuticals 5% → 4.7%, Metal-Materials 3.8% → 5.9%, and Hotel-Real Property 0.4% → 3.9%.

Figure 5 The emergence of new sectors for mainland Chinese investments in Europe, 2003–2009

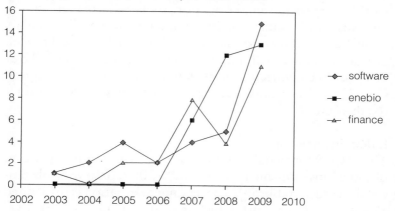

Source: Authors' database.

Note: enebio – Energy and BioChemicals.

The stability of the textile-clothing sector's share and fashion-related activities reflect the numerous acquisitions made in luxury goods by Chinese firms. It mirrors the emergence of a sustained consumer demand in China driven by prestigious brands. France and the United Kingdom receive nearly 60 per cent of these investments and the Li & Fung Group is particularly bustling (see case study 4).

The significant investments in banking and finance sectors stem from the UK appeal, despite the crisis: over three-quarters of these investments are located in this country. The Bank of China is a prominent investor.

Hong Kong investment is focused on the textile-clothing sector, transport and logistics and, to a lesser extent, hotel and real property. This positioning reflects the traditional comparative advantages of Hong Kong – even if textiles and clothing are now produced in adjacent provinces of mainland China – and in specialized transport and warehousing services, as illustrated by the activity of the Hutchison Whampoa conglomerate which is continuing to expand in the perfumery

37

sector (especially in the United Kingdom), and in dock work and port facilities through Hutchison Port Holdings, the world's largest terminal operator. Its last European venture involves an investment of approximately 800 million dollars to built a container terminal at Fos/Port de Marseille (France). The new terminal will start commercial operations in 2017 or 2018 and be connected to its 'sister terminal', the European Container Terminal, located in the Port of Rotterdam (Netherlands).

Indian investments

The ITC sector remains dominant in Europe with 28 per cent of Indian investments made in 2008–2009, despite a substantial downturn (table 5b). The leading destination is the United Kingdom (53 per cent), which is strengthening its attractiveness. It is well ahead of Germany (16 per cent), France (12 per cent) and Central European countries (10 per cent); all three areas have seen their drawing power crumble since 2002.

The chemical and pharmaceutical sectors follow well behind (12.5 per cent of investments for the same period). This last sector has also lost ground, but less than the previous one. The main destination countries are the United Kingdom (22 per cent), which has eased back compared with the previous period, and Germany (22 per cent), with the reverse trend, then Italy (19 per cent) which has gained several places and has thus moved ahead of Central European countries and France (11 per cent each).

The third place is occupied by the banking and finance sectors (12 per cent). The crisis does not seem to have affected the investment decisions in the banking and finance sectors: the results are investments of somehow contra-cyclical nature. There are two explanations: projects scheduled before the crisis and maintained – which seems to confirm the major share occupied by creating branches or subsidiaries as is the case for the ICICI Bank, among others – or the crisis has created new opportunities in this sector in Europe.

Then comes the equipment sector which is on the rise (11.5

Table 5b   Sectoral distribution of Indian investments, 2008–2009 versus 2000–2007 (in number)[7]

Sectors/Periods	2008–2009	
ITC, including:	59	
Information processing, Software, Consultancy		*56*
Telecommunications		*3*
Chemicals and Pharmaceuticals	26	
Chemicals		*6*
Pharmaceuticals		*20*
Car manufacture	21	
Bank-Finance	25	
Equipment	24	
Metal work	8	
Transport-Logistics	11	
Materials	8	
Textile-Clothing	7	
Food processing	6	

Source: Authors' database.

per cent) when compared to the previous period. Electrical and electronic equipments are the main component.

It is just followed by car manufacture (10 per cent), which is also rising. This is equally surprising given the severity of the crisis in this sector with no sub-sector of the European automotive industry being spared. The many closures of European sites, including those acquired previously by Indian firms, may have discouraged new arrivals. The main destination countries are the United Kingdom (33 per cent) and Germany (24 per cent). Germany dropped back, however, during the crisis years, ceding its previous leadership to the United Kingdom, which exhibits a surprising attractiveness in

7 For information, we indicate the relative shares of the concerned Indian activities before and since 2008: ITC 40.6% → 28.4%, Chemical-Pharmaceuticals 19.5% → 12.5%, Car manufacture 7.9% → 10.1%, Bank-Finance 3.4% → 12%, Equipment 9.9% → 11.5%, Metal work 4.9% → 3.8%, Transport-Logistics 1.3% → 5.3%, Materials 2.4% → 3.8%, Textile-Clothing 4.5% → 3.4%, and Food processing 3.5% → 2.9%.

this activity sector when one knows the deindustrialisation level reached by the UK economy across the board.

3.3 The crisis provided opportunities for Chinese and Indian investors in some sectors and activities

If the financial crisis had negative impacts, as documented previously, on Chinese and Indian investments carried out in Europe, the crisis also provided new opportunities. Some empirical evidence can be put forward either in sectors with an established presence or in new ones. These include:

For both investors:
(a)   the rise in the European car manufacture sector,
(b)   the set up of numerous bank branches and other establishments by financial institutions.
For Chinese firms:
(c)   the emergence of a truly software sector,
(d)   the move up the value chain of textile-clothing,
(e)   the breakthrough of investments in renewable energies,
(f)   lastly, the opportunities offered by setting up in Central European countries will be re-assessed in the light of a case study of the main Chinese investment made in the Czech Republic (see Box 6).

The remaining of the section will be nurtured by selected case studies which detail the investment decision and the resulting strategies by most representative Chinese and Indian investors in Europe.

3.3.1   Rising investments in the European automotive sector

Both Chinese and Indian investors are here involved.

Chinese investments

The crisis had a dual impact on the Chinese automotive sector. Firstly, it propelled China into first place worldwide in terms of production and market, and secondly, it altered the competition that had been raging so far between China and the industrialised world. The new balance of powers was shaped by two underlying forces: a successful accumulation of knowledge through frequently contacts with world car manufacturers over the last decade on one side, and the capability of Chinese firms to satisfy increasingly 'good enough' markets at world level, whilst making ground-breaking progress in electric vehicles on the other. This new trend opened the way for Chinese firms in the sector to acquire abroad firms in difficulty or being dismantled at affordable prices when compared with prices in previous years. Similarly, the crisis incited Chinese firms to free themselves from foreign dependency in terms of technology and recognised brands by acquiring in Europe (and the United States) expertise they had been lacking until then, which had hampered their domestic development and also their international expansion.

There was therefore no surprise in Chinese firms taking a stance on every deal of automotive businesses in Europe since the end of 2008.

This strategy can be illustrated with a few examples picked up for the sole year 2009:

- Three Chinese manufacturers (Geely, Chery and Chang'An) took a clear stance on the takeover of the Swedish manufacturer Volvo, a subsidiary of Ford Motors. The offer finally adopted was from Geely, which had already acquired the UK company Manganese Bronze in 2007. The initial intention was to maintain production in Sweden.
- Beijing Automotive Industry Holding/BAIC showed interest in taking over Opel (subsidiary of General Motors) before its rapid elimination.

- The same company was associated on a minority equity engagement with the small, luxury Swedish car manufacturer Koenigsegg to take over the other Swedish manufacturer, Saab (a General Motors subsidiary). Ultimately, Koenigsegg withdrew from the transaction which was therefore cancelled.
- BAIC reacted immediately and decided to continue alone, showing interest to take over part of the group's assets. But the Swedish authorities had no desire to see the Saab know-how and reputation going to China and therefore rejected the new proposal. A Dutch luxury car manufacturer, Spyker Cars, finally bought out Saab. Most European economic commentators expressed their satisfaction that the emblematic Swedish company had been taken over by a European company. This viewpoint cannot turn its back on reality, as over 50 per cent of the Spyker capital is held by non-European institutions investors (30 per cent by the Russian financial group Convers and 25 per cent by the Abu Dhabi sovereign fund, Mubadala Development Co.).
- The car engineering firm Dr Qu Li's Eco Concept Ltd., with its close links with Shanghai Automotive Industry Corp. (SAIC), the first Chinese car manufacturer, bought out the assets of the UK van producer, DV (Birmingham) in October 2009 and transferred production lines to China (Shanghai). A presence was nevertheless maintained in the United Kingdom at the Longbridge site where SAIC was already operating after the acquisition of Rover in 2007.
- The bus manufacturer Xiamen King Long United Automotive Industry decided to set up an assembly plant in Hungary in December 2009.
- Lastly, it must be underlined that BYD, which took the decision to launch its electric car models onto the US market in 2010 (with Warren Buffet), intends subsequently to get a foot in the European market. BYD also created at the start of 2010 a strategic partnership with

the German group Daimler to design an electric version of the Class A model car.

Indian investments

Like China, the Indian automotive sector is driven by a booming domestic market, and investments abroad are for a large part intended to acquire skills to bolster local production units.

Over half the Indian automotive investments in Europe are bound to two countries – the United Kingdom and Germany. The aim is to acquire universally-known brands, car parts manufacturers or even test consumer reactions by putting on the market radically new products like electric cars. Tata Motors straddles these different strategies: indeed, it acquired Jaguar and Land Rover brands in early 2008, took a majority stake in a small Norwegian manufacturer of electric cars (Miljo Grenland) the same year, and further launched the development of a new electric model in its Warwick research centre with the support of the UK Government.

If the number of Indian acquisition decreased in 2009 they have rebounded in 2010, mainly trough the acquisition of numerous auto part manufacturers not only in the UK and Germany but also in Belgium, the Czech Republic, Italy and the Netherlands. The interest in European tyre manufacturers is also confirmed through two new acquisitions.

3.3.2   The creation of numerous bank branches and other financial establishments by Chinese and Indian companies

Similarly to the car industry, both Chinese and Indian bank and financial companies are concerned with fairly close motivations and strategies: first, to follow and support the presence of national client firms, second, to develop deposit activities or become familiar with distinctive management practices and national and regional context (Eurozone).

Chinese investments

The major Chinese public banks all have branches in the main European countries. They are not simply aiming to support the arrival of their client firms in Europe, but to acquire new expertise in follow-up relations with customers and in management standards.

The current crisis has not altered this trend, for Chinese banks in particular have continued to arrive in Europe over the past two years.

The increased attractiveness of the United Kingdom for Chinese investments in this sector must be underlined, particularly the place of London. China Merchants Bank, China UnionPay and China Reinsurance chose London in 2009 for their first European set ups, whilst the China Construction Bank and the Agricultural Bank of China expanded their London activity. The Bank of China, which currently has branches in five English cities, started up a new deposit bank activity in 2009 with highly-competitive loans and an advantageous positioning in the mortgage market, with rates some 2.5 per cent to 3.5 per cent less than the Bank of England rates. In 2010, the Industrial and Commercial Bank of China[8] is embarking on a new venture in Europe – the opening of four branches for deposit bank transactions. At the same time it is planning to create a world foreign exchange transaction centre in London in conjunction with its Beijing and New York centres, thereby providing a seamless service for its customers.

Lastly, mention can be made of portfolio investments[9] made in Europe by the China Investment Corp. (CIC), the Chinese sovereign wealth fund which is mandated to manage part of China's large foreign exchange reserves, as several European companies have been targeted. For example, the CIC is part of a consortium which has recently bailed out a London office complex (Canary Wharf) to the tune of 1.3 billion dollars

8 ICBC's earnings rank No. 1 among all listed banks in the world.
9 The value of the equity must be less than 10 per cent of the capital of the company involved.

following the company's recapitalisation. It also made a minority equity investment in Glencore (raw materials trader, Switzerland) and in Diageo (spirits, United Kingdom) in 2009 for an amount of 365 million Euros. In May 2010, the CIC made an equity investment in the French perfumery company, L'Occitane.

Indian investments

Indian investors in this sector have not lagged behind. The vast majority of the operations identified are destined to the United Kingdom: private banks (e.g. ICICI), public banks (State Bank of India) and financial institutions specialising in real property, leasing and external trade are concerned. In 2009, greenfield operations are quite the sole mode of entry due to numerous branches opened across the United Kingdom by Indian banks. In 2010, the geographical scope of acquisitions made by Indian banks and financial institution were extended to Germany and Luxemburg.

3.3.3   The emergence of a truly software sector by Chinese firms

Until the last two years, it was well vaunted that the Indians tended to specialise in software whilst hardware was reserved for the Chinese. This distinction is still true, but is changing.

It seems that the crisis has spurred Chinese software firms to make more effort to catch up their Indian counterpart already well established in Europe. Beijing, Nanjing-Jiangsu and Dalian in particular – as home of a technological software centre whose development was driven by sub-contractor tasks to large Japanese companies – are extremely ambitious and

10 This notion refers to the use of memory and computing capacities of computers in a networked context. End-users no longer own their IT services but access online services as and when required without having to manage the underlying infrastructure. Software as a service (SaaS) is a concept that offers a subscription to software instead of purchasing a licence.

embarked on a strategy of emulating Bangalore, the *Silicon Valley* of India, within the next years.

The Chinese software firms are targeting *niche* markets in a booming global sector whilst market perspectives are increasingly driven by 'virtualisation' and cloud computing[10] to reduce costs and increase efficiency. To be sure, Chinese companies have cost advantages over industrial countries in outsourcing. According to China Software Industry, the market for this activity was 2.7 billion dollars in 2009, with a projected market of 6.9 billion dollars in 2013. The Chinese outsourcing market has more than tripled between 2007 and 2009 to reach 20 billion dollars and, according to KPMG, China replaced India last year as the outsourcing destination for firms in the Asia-Pacific area.[11] Nevertheless, Chinese firms still have to prove themselves internationally, as for the moment they are still disadvantaged compared with Indian firms: they are less familiar with English and business environments, and sub-contracting service operators are slightly wary of them (fear of pirated data, of providing information to the Chinese Government, etc.).

As in the case of the banking sector, the United Kingdom has been a conspicuous recipient since 2008. For example, the plan is for about 100 small Chinese firms to open offices in the United Kingdom by 2012, especially in London with the prospect of the forthcoming Summer Olympic Games. These dynamics follow on from experiences of the previous Olympics held in Beijing in 2008. A few flagship firms deserve a mention: VanceInfo Technologies, Crystal Digital, Insigma, Geong, Uni-Ta Technology, Evoc Intelligent, eBaoTech and Honay. They provide a full range of information technology, communication and design services.

We are now going to focus on the investments made in Europe by three emblematic Chinese software firms: Alibaba.com, Neusoft and eBaoTech.

11 According to *China Daily*, 15/07/2010.

Case study 1
Alibaba.com lands in Europe
Alibaba.com was born with the millennium and, in just a few years, has become the world e-commerce and B-to-B market specialist for small and medium-sized companies. The fledgling firm, with 39 per cent of its capital held by Yahoo, has been quoted on the Hong Kong stock exchange since 2007 and currently claims 40 million users worldwide. The firm operates on the call centre model, putting thousands of businesses, principals, providers of manufactured products, raw materials, materials, varied services, etc. into contact with one another.

Overseas markets today account for 60 per cent of the group's income (USA, India and the United Kingdom come first), and the firm aims to expand into Europe from its sales offices located in Switzerland (2007) and the United Kingdom (2008). Besides, Alibaba.com opened its European headquarters in London in September 2009. The office created 14 initial jobs and is also responsible for the African and Middle-Eastern markets. The choice of London can be explained by the presence of its first clientele – 450,000 in 2009 with 2,000 new customers every week. The other reasons given are the United Kingdom's openness to the outside, its cultural diversity and its major advancement in the digital economy and advertising: indeed, 2/3 of international advertising agencies are headquartered in London. The directors of the Chinese company believe that success in the United Kingdom largely conditions their success at the European level. This investment is nevertheless a challenge for Alibaba.com, as the firm is little-known in Europe, but the widespread advertising campaign (TV commercials and posters on London taxis for an amount of 30 million dollars) when setting up the European headquarters hints at the firm's ambition to increase brand name recognition and make its presence felt in Europe.

Case study 2
Neusoft chooses Switzerland as its European expansion base
Neusoft stands for NorthEastern University SOFTware. It is

a leading IT services and software company in China. Neusoft Europe's headquarters are in Switzerland (Zurich), where it proposes to create a R&D, design, production and sales subsidiary. The firm stands out from its counterparts through the acquisitions it has already made in Europe to increase its know-how in product engineering and speed up its world market penetration. Neusoft acquired the Finnish company Sesca in September 2009 (250 employees), a specialist in mobile telephone software and its three Romanian subsidiaries. Although Neusoft abandoned its plan to set up business in Hungary following the crisis, it is seeking to acquire VND Bus & Asts, a subsidiary of the German company Harman.

Case study 3
The European rise of eBaoTech
This firm, specialising in the insurance software sector (life insurance, home insurance, accident insurance, etc.), is worth the detour for it is not an activity where you would normally expect Chinese presence in Europe. China does not have the same huge tradition of insurance as Europe and has not, so far, really taken a stance in software development, unlike India.

eBaotech was founded in Shanghai in 2000 and has grown rapidly since then (40 per cent per year on average). The company is currently run by 3 people (two Chinese and one Swiss). It employs 900 people in the world, has clients in 20 countries and pools its resources with a network of companies, including the Indian Hexaware, HCL and Mahindra System, the Australian iTree and the French Cap Gemini. eBaoTech has two foreign subsidiaries, one in Singapore and the other in Switzerland.

The firm's activity is structured around major geographical divisions, each one with its own employees in Shanghai, and

12 The Swiss Chairman and Managing Director, Mr Adamec, is a shareholder.

mixed teams are therefore found in each region. The firm has been present in Europe since 2004 as a Chinese-Swiss joint venture[12] headquartered in Zurich. It manages all the group's European activities as well as the Indian and African business.

eBaotech has an office in Rotterdam (Netherlands) since 2008 covering the Benelux market and another office in Birmingham (United Kingdom) focusing entirely on the local market. The firm is fully integrated with the European insurance software industry and is reputed for its skills.

eBaoTech Europe currently has 110 employees, including 30 in Europe (20 in Zurich, 8 in Rotterdam and 2 in Birmingham), 60 in China (Shanghai) and 20 in India.

The firm originally set up in Europe to meet its ever-increasing customer numbers. Switzerland was chosen for its position as a financial and linguistic crossroads; Zurich is very diverse linguistically – German is spoken, of course, as are French and English. The fact that the joint director of eBaoTech is a Swiss national also played a part, and the Swiss Department of Immigration was supportive in quickly issuing visas for its Chinese personnel.

eBaoTech offers a mix of skills and optimised task distribution to exploit a *niche* activity involving highly-customised, top-end and complex services. It takes on average five months to two years to set up a new service.

eBaoTech is extremely autonomous despite its close relations with the Shanghai headquarters and the development offices located in China and India. The headquarters provides the overall group strategy and defines the development of projects and how they are financed, whilst eBaoTech Europe manages the projects, sells their products and deals with customer relations.

The firm makes quality a priority and currently a mere 10 per cent of its business is in China, as its directors state that the market is more restricted than in Europe. In addition, strong competition pushes prices and the quality of products on offer downwards. The firm is seeking recognition through a customised, monitored approach with its international customers and does not therefore fear competition from Indian firms with their more global approach. Substantial investments are constantly made in staff training.

Having said that, its directors acknowledge the challenge facing a Chinese firm specialising in software and they are forever portraying a quality image for their services, to the point of erasing their Chinese origin.

3.3.4 The climbing of the value chain for the Chinese textile-clothing sector

The financial crisis affected the Chinese textile-clothing sector in many ways, a sector that had become a dominant actor worldwide, particularly through exports. The resurgence of this sector was largely due to foreign partnerships and subcontracting operations from large Western and Japanese groups (large clothing companies and retailers) seeking the lowest possible production costs, particularly low wages and high productivity in a still labour-intensive sector.

The crisis had an initial impact on final demand, located mainly in Europe and the United States, which endangered firms at the end of the chain. Some small manufacturers did not survive. However, the resultant restructuring of the sector has boosted the survivors, helped them grow their market shares, carried out economies of scale and implemented new ways of increasing R&D, to innovate, improve the design of their products, push their own brands forward and, ultimately, raise the production value. Such an industrial rebirth is totally in line with the objectives of Chinese public authorities which wish to reduce the share of the textile sector in domestic production and give up sewing tasks. They are now seeking to move national production up the chain value,

13 This is confirmed by a recent survey by the consultancy firm Jassin O'Rourke (USA).

promote research and use new fibres with the aim to improve their returns. The bottom-end industries are now even less featured as labour costs are rising, despite the huge reserves of manpower in inland China. The 'bottom-end' textile firms are therefore increasingly battered by competition from other Asian countries with lower labour costs (Vietnam and Bangladesh especially):[13] the average hourly wage for a Chinese worker is 1.08 dollar in the coastal provinces and 0.55 to 0.80 in the inland provinces. The hourly wage in India is 0.51 dollar, whilst Bangladesh posts the lowest wage of all, about one-fifth of wage levels in Shanghai and Suzhou.[14]

The crisis has also weakened many Western textile-clothing groups through falling sales and new difficulties in getting their customers to pay or in getting new bank loans. Many have gone into liquidation, thereby freeing up buyout opportunities for potential investors, including Chinese.

Many Chinese firms in the textile-clothing and fashion sector have now reached a turning point and wish to transform their activity with a strategy of international expansion via exports and/or by locating abroad. They have the resources to finance their ambitions, are often supported by Chinese public authorities and make the most of the opening up of European markets following the Multi Fibre Arrangement of 1 January 2005. Lastly, they have solid managerial and productive skills acquired mainly over the last two decades through frequent contact with their Western partners and principals.

The crisis has not shattered the momentum of Chinese investments made in the textile-clothing sector in Europe since the start of the millennium; at most it has changed the behaviours and strategies towards increased professionalization.

France and the United Kingdom lead the way for greenfields. New Chinese firms, mainly from the mainland, are seeking a presence in Europe as part of their growth strategy. Some have no hesitation in promoting their own brands,

14 Ang Yuen Yuen, Renewal of 'Made in China', *Les Echos*, 8/06/2010.

which is new. The Mouse Ji haute couture workshop in Paris and the LF Beauty formulation laboratories in London and Paris are two such examples.

The subsidiary created in France (Saint-Amarin) by a joint venture between the Zhonghe group (cotton spinner, manufacturer of fabrics and finished products from Fujian) and the Velcorex-BKC group (a spin-off from DMC) to produce fabrics intended for the Chinese market under a 'reverse delocalisation' strategy, is worth being underlined in a sector which has delocalised to China so extensively in the past. The small production of fabrics runs from 2011 onwards will be intended for Chinese designers seeking fabrics 'made in France', and for Chinese brands and stores on the lookout for innovative fabrics standing out from basic ranges.[15]

The acquisitions of European firms in the textile-clothing sector – there have been many since the crisis – cover in all cases companies having been in distress. These transactions initiated by mainland or Hong Kong firms, have mainly involved the United Kingdom (way out ahead), France and Italy. As expected, Switzerland remains in the lead for watch making buyouts: for instance, Milus watches now belong to Chow Tai Fook and Chouriet watches to Fiyta Ltd.

A few examples of symbolic acquisitions, often at the top-end of the sector, stand out during the 2008–2010 period.

In the United Kingdom, the acquisitions of:

- Todd & Ducan (luxury cashmere, 200 employees, founded 142 years ago) by Ningxia Zhingyin Cashmere for 6 million pounds from a UK firm Dawson International, that the group had tried to buy out unsuccessfully one year before. This is an example of a buyout by a subcontractor of a former participant (5 years relationship) working in a luxury sector, with recognised know-how and a famous brand. Ningxia Zhingyin

15 See O. Opin, Saic Velcorex carries out cross-transactions with the Chinese Zhonghe (http://ydmconsultants.com/pdf/ZH-SAIC_JV_JDT.pdf).

decided to keep production in Scotland to preserve the accumulated knowledge, as well as for consumer reassurance via the 'made in Scotland' label;
- Three clothing companies (Hardy Amies, Kent & Curwen, and Visage by Li & Fung);
- Lulu Guiness (luxury leather bags) by First Eastern Financial;
- Shelly Shoes (Converse, Kickers, Gola, Crocs brands, etc.) by Eternal Best Industries (Hong Kong);
- Greenwoods Menswear (leisure clothes) by Bosideng via its subsidiary Harvest Fancy (556 employees and 87 outlets), up to 50 per cent for 50 million pounds.

In France, the buyouts of:
- Solala by Golife Concept (Hong Kong);
- the property rights of Pierre Cardin name for the whole of China (including Taiwan and Macao) by Zhongfu (Shanghai), and Pierre Cardin licences for leather shoes and accessories of the group for 200 million Euros by Guangzhou Jiansheng Trading. In fact, the consequences of such buyouts are similar to the entire firm being bought out, all the more so as it now finds itself totally dismantled.[16]

Lastly, in Italy, the buyout of Sergio Tacchini (sportswear) by Hembly (Hong Kong), specialized in sub-contracting and distributing textile products.

Case study 4
The Acquisitions by the Li & Fung Group in Europe
The strategy adopted by Li & Fung in Europe is interesting by

16 For information, the Pierre Cardin group was one of the first foreign groups to set up in China in 1978 and the first Western fashion designer to parade in Beijing. At the end of 2008, two other firms, Jiangsheng Trading and Cardanro, had already sought to buy out the Pierre Cardin clothing group unsuccessfully.
17 And to a lesser extent in toys, sports goods and fireworks.

itself and also as it is typical of strategies adopted by numerous Chinese firms wishing to climb the chain value.

The firm first learned from outsourcing, mainly in the textile and accessories sector,[17] gravitating over the years to different stages in the value chain before today coordinating all its tasks. This progress went with on-going improvement of the quality of products and services proposed, at the same time as an external growth strategy in the United States and Europe which gave it clientele and new production capacities, well-known brands and quality labels.

Today, Li & Fung is selling more and more under its own brand and that of bought-out firms or licences, a long way from its original core business.

Box 2   The Li & Fung Group

The firm was founded in Canton in 1906 to export goods (silk, porcelain, bamboo, craft goods, fireworks), and rapidly opened an office in the port of Hong Kong to better control its shipments. After 1949 and the advent of the Mao era, the firm set up definitively in Hong Kong from where it exported goods (clothing, toys, plastic items, etc.) manufactured in the City State, mainly towards the United States and Asia. The opening up of mainland China in 1978 and the massive delocalisation there of Hong Kong factories marked the start of a sourcing business for the firm. Its customer network expanded step by step and its trade expertise increased. The firm then diversified into retail trade (mid-1980s) following equity investments of 50 per cent in two Hong Kong store chains (Circle K and Toys R).

The mid-1990s saw the firm become truly international with, in particular, the acquisition of the English firm Inchcape Buying Services-Dodwell in 1995, which helped extend its networks into Europe and India. The firm then expanded into the American and African continents before embarking on a highly-aggressive external growth strategy with the new millennium by acquiring Swire and Maclaine (Hong Kong), Camberley (China) and Colby Group, its main competitor, followed by others in North America and in Europe (like the German group KarstadtQuelle).

Li & Fung has built its reputation on the quality of its services and its ability to provide the best quality-price ratio to its customers. Its directors very quickly learned to optimise their services, supplies and the added value of their products by calling on different partners selected for the advantages of their production sites. This type of strategy remains the cornerstone of the group's expertise and the specific features of its services. It also helps maintain customer loyalty.

Li & Fung has become the world leader of outsourcing in textile-clothing and includes renowned customers like Marks & Spencer, Wal-Mart, Zara, Esprit, Mexx, Target and Gap. Its business now covers the entire clothing and accessory sector whilst the group manages the major world brands. These include Calvin Klein, Timberland, Disney, Marvel, Warner Brothers, Hasbro, Marvel (since its buyout of the American group Wear Me Apparel at the end of 2009, specialized in children's clothes and image-wear, for 401 million dollars).

Li & Fung is run by two brothers, Victor and William Fung, third-generation descendants of the firm's founder. It employs 13,400 people worldwide and its turnover reached 20 billion dollars in 2010.

Li & Fung made a fairly high number of buyouts since 2008. It has capitalised on opportunities to acquire local firms with numerous advantages whilst seeking less dependence on the North American market, which accounts for nearly two-thirds of its turnover. These transactions have benefited a billion-dollar endowment capital from the firm's directors in 2008. In fact, the vast majority of European acquisitions involve companies in financial difficulties, especially in the

United Kingdom and Germany. In the former Li & Fung acquired the following companies:

- Hardy Amies, official supplier of clothes to the Queen for nearly 50 years;
- Kent & Curwen, a London manufacturer of luxury men's goods through a minority equity investment. This includes brands like Altea, Cerruti 1881, D'Urban, Gieves & Hawkes and Intermezzo;
- Visage (Manchester, 500 employees), specialised in the manufacture of clothes for the wholesale textile trade (264 million dollars).

In Germany, the group bought out Miles Fashion (51 million dollars), a specialist in ready-to-wear and sports clothes with a solid retailer network (80 outlets in 40 countries). This firm does not have its own factories and sub-contracts all its production to China, Bangladesh and Singapore.

Li & Fung also created a European subsidiary, LF Beauty, in 2009. This company specialises in beauty products and cosmetics, with establishments in the United Kingdom and France. It was somehow the final piece in the group's strategic development puzzle, a combination of domestic know-how and the desire for a European showcase. LF Beauty sees itself as a global service provider throughout the 'beauty' sector utilising a vast network of skills. LF Beauty thus incorporates the commercial resources of the group in Europe (Paris and London), the United States (New York and Dallas) and China, a formulation laboratory in the United Kingdom, product development, sourcing, project management and quality assurance teams and filling units (United Kingdom and China). The various teams manage thousands of suppliers and manufacturing partners along an integrated business.

3.3.5   The breakthrough by Chinese investments in renewable energies

The renewable energy sector has seen strong growth in China over the past five years. Indeed, the Chinese authorities have become aware of the seriousness of climate change and the risk therefore weighing on the development of the economy and Chinese society with the on-going, sustained increase in domestic energy demand propelled by the country's rise in living standards and unbridled urbanisation. The Chinese authorities are therefore promoting the exploitation of cleaner, less polluting energy sources and reducing its reliance on foreign supplies.

It makes economic sense to consider how China has modified its use of renewable energies in recent years, especially since the crisis, before examining the new situation.

Following the implementation in 2005 of the law on renewable energies providing for a 40 per cent to 45 per cent reduction in greenhouse gas emissions by 2020, investments have increased in this sector by an extraordinary annual rate of 144 per cent. In 2009 alone, China injected 34.6 billion dollars into 'green' energies compared with the United States' 18.6 billion. In just a few years, the country has increased its renewable energy contribution to 52.5 gigawatts, mainly through the wind power and biomass sectors. This equates to 52 medium-sized coal-fired power plants.

China became the world's leading automotive market in 2009, highlighted by the use of electric, hybrid or small-cylinder vehicles with low fuel consumption. The Chinese authorities have just introduced on 1 June 2010 discounts on purchases of these 'green' vehicles.[18] China is intending to include radical measures in the 12th Five-Year Plan (2011–2015) to encourage the use of a wide range of energies.

---

18 About 360 Euros for vehicles with less than 1.6 litre engine capacity, purchase tax of 7.5 per cent instead of 10 per cent combined with a subsidy granted for the purchase of an electric vehicle.

Box 3 Renewable energy production and use inventories in China

China is planning for an installed nuclear power capacity of 86 gigawatts (gW) by 2020, up nearly 10-fold from the 9 gW capacity it had by the end of 2008.

In 2009, the effective production capacity of hydraulic plants reached 197 gW, thereby becoming the world leader. This has reduced carbon dioxide emissions by 520 million tonnes.

Wind power doubled between 2006 and 2008, achieving 12.2 gW. In 2009, it exceeded 22 gW, moving China into third place in the world.

The country is also the leader in solar panels and in photovoltaic battery power, with an annual accumulated production of 4 gW, i.e. 40 per cent of world production.

In 2009, the installed capacity of biomass power plants reached 4.5 gW, including 2 gW produced from straw and 0.5 gW from refuse. China currently has 35 million households with methane-generating wells and 1,500 methane structures in the large cattle rearing centres. All together they produce 15 billion cubic meters of methane a year.

Lastly, bio fuels are expanding and the techniques and industrialisation of other energy sources are taking their first steps.

China's development in this sector relies on cooperation with Europe to develop new energy sources and activities gravitating around energy savings. Thus, various Chinese investments are already visible in Europe in this sector. Although many of the Chinese firms involved are frequently looking to expand their sales offices, some of them are also seeking to tap specific know-how. This concern is clear, for example, in the large-scale investment carried out by State

Grid and Dragon Power in Sweden. Established in a forest region in the North of Sweden, the project aims at producing ethanol at industrial scale from raw materials like wood, peat, straw and hemp.

The cellulose is converted into sugar by a chemical process involving sulphuric acid, then the sugar is fermented to produce alcohol, which in turn is distilled and purified and ultimately produces ethanol to fuel cars. Biogas is also produced from by-products of the distillery. The project, called National Bio Energy, is a joint venture between the two large Chinese companies and a Swedish firm. The operation benefits from major public financing: European, Swedish and regional (Jämtland county). It is also supported academically through a partnership forged with the University of Lund.

Chinese firms have also been active in wind energy and photovoltaic panels both inside and outside their country, mainly in the United States and Europe. Most of their European investments take the form of sales offices. In a

---

Box 4   Xinjiang Goldwind Science and Technology

The firm is specialized in the building and operation of wind farms. It set up its first fields in 1998 in the Chinese provinces of Xinjiang and Hebei. Goldwind is second in its sector in China (behind Sinovel) and fifth in the world.

The firm employs 1,500 people. It is listed on the Shenzhen Stock Exchange and anticipates being listed in Hong Kong to raise new funds to finance further investments. It has sales offices in Australia and the United States where it could ultimately install production units.

The corporate development is supported by the Chinese State: in 2009 it received 7 million Euros of public aid and also enjoyed preferential rate bank loans.

context of crisis and overproduction of this sector in Europe, Chinese investments are weakening European firms, especially in Germany, all the more so as these new investors are supported extensively by their state and resort to attractive call prices (see Box 3).

The wind energy sector is also a priority for redeployment in China towards other primary energy sources. The resulting emergence of domestic producers is not restricted to supplying the domestic market only and an increasing number are exporting or even creating foreign subsidiaries.

Xinjiang Goldwind (also named Goldwind) is the main Chinese investor in Europe in this sector due to a majority equity stake in Vensys (Germany) in 2008. The production and R&D activities were maintained in Germany.

The Goldwind wind turbines, which are manufactured in Germany, promote a quality label with prices 20 per cent to 30 per cent lower than those quoted by the European competition, due to the use of components manufactured in China and Chinese public aid.

In addition, Chinese groups are currently involved in setting up several solar farms in Europe (Romania and Spain in particular). Otherwise, there are many Chinese investors in the photovoltaic sector, mostly in sales activities, as follows. Germany is the first European recipient for Chinese investment in this sector. Some examples:

- Suntech Power, whose activity is mainly overseas (80 per cent of its turnover in 2008 and 2009), has grown quickly after acquiring the Japanese firm MSK and the North American firm MCEM. In 2008 and 2009, Suntech Power set up its European headquarters in Switzerland to coordinate the activity of its German, Spanish, French, Italian and Greek sales subsidiaries.
- Sky Global, part of the Shanghai Electric group, which is building a photovoltaic panel factory in Spain (Mataporquera, Cantabria) scheduled to be operated in 2011 (14.5 million Euros and 465 planned jobs);

Box 5 Yingli Green Energy

Created in 1998 and today is one of the top ten world solar panel manufacturers. It employs 6,000 people at its headquarters in Baoding and is listed on the New York Stock Exchange.

Yingli's main claim to fame is its integration of all production stages (ingots, wafers, cells and solar modules). The company reached high standards of quality through numerous controls.

The group opened a sale office in Lyon in late 2009. Its first French customer was EDF Energies Nouvelles. GDF Suez is expected to place an order shortly for 145,000 panels to be assembled in a ground solar plant with a power of 32 megawatts, to be set up in Curbans (Alpes-de-Haute-Provence).

It was also the first renewable energy firm to sponsor the 2010 FIFA World Cup (South Africa) and the first Chinese company to sign a global sponsoring contract with the world soccer governing body.

- Yingli Green Energy has made several investments in Europe (France, Germany and Italy) due to an existent large customer base.

Without being exhaustive, mention can be made of investments by Zhejiang BLD Solar Technology, a firm created in June 2008 and already making its presence felt in the German, Italian and Spanish markets. Added to that are the investments by LDK Solar in Germany and Italy, and by UP Solar in France.

Other Chinese investors are beginning to offer their services in Europe as energy saving solutions. For example, China Super Power Saving, which has just expanded further into Europe by creating two companies in France: CSPS European Energy Savings (Neuilly-sur-Seine) with a forecast of fifteen jobs, and World Energy Saving Solutions, specialising in promoting urban and public energy saving projects (car parks, metro, airport, warehouses). The firm has just set up a distribution network for its products in Germany, Switzerland and Italy. It is aiming to head the energy savings market in Europe within five years based on an original business model: installing its products free of charge and sharing with the customer firm the profits from reducing the electricity bill over a five-to seven-year period.

3.3.6 A new look at installations in the Central European countries

The enlargement of the European Union in 2004 and 2007 to include Bulgaria, Hungary, Poland, the Czech Republic, Romania and Slovakia has without doubt stimulated economic activity in this area, until then on the sidelines of the Union. Chinese and Indian investors saw there a new opportunity to broaden their local market shares and a springboard to serve and penetrate neighbouring Western European markets, whilst taking advantage of lower labour costs, less strict social constraints and specific aids from the European Union, with tax exemptions on investments of up to 40 per cent over ten years.

The outcome of all these investments is somewhat mixed, however.

The state of political and diplomatic relations had a decisive influence on the choice of location, in particular for Chinese investments. As a result, Poland, Romania or Hungary, which enjoy excellent relations with China, are more attractive for Chinese investment than the Czech Republic, whose political relations with the People's Republic of China are far less cordial.

The first results from the dataset show up a clearer impact of the financial crisis on new Chinese and Indian investment projects in this area. The production and assembly activities were most affected: several investments programmed in 2007 or early 2008 could not ultimately be executed. To that is added the closure of some production units set up in 2004–2005, or some of them being delocalised to developing countries. Furthermore, the assembly activities locations have been rationalized. For example, Hisense closed its factory in Hungary in 2009 and re-opened it in Egypt. Lenovo, after various rumours of closure and hesitations, finally gave up the idea of investing in Poland to choose Mexico. Lastly, BYD Electronic, which has halved its workforce in Hungary where it had set up in 2008 following its buyout of the local group Mirae, has also pulled out of producing in Romania. Admittedly, these investments concerned the telephone sector whereas the group is now focusing on electric car production, partly due to the crisis which has opened up new prospects in this sector.

Some Indian investors have also been forced to review their Central European investment projects, like the tyre manufacturer, Apollo Tyres, which decided through 2008 not to continue with its tyre factory project planned to be built in Hungary, whereas in 2009 it acquired a Dutch tyre manufacturer, Vredestein Banden.

Overall, Chinese investors are looking beyond the negative effects of the crisis and re-assessing the place of Central European countries in their installation and extension strategy at European scale. As stated above, these investors have not only become more careful and patient, but also more attuned to the reputation of the origin of their productions and the quality of their products. They are aware that producing with a 'made in Poland' or a 'made in Hungary' label has less appeal than a 'made in France, in Germany or in the UK.' Besides, they are well aware that the Central European formalities are frequently more costly than in Western Europe. By way of illustration, Chinese immigration is banned in the Czech Republic.

All things considered, the Central European markets are no less attractive for Chinese and Indian investors, as their consumers have living standards which are reasonably comparable with those of the rising middle-classes in their own countries. Moreover, they constitute a learning opportunity and a first experience abroad: see, for example, in Romania the recent set up of a tractor assembly plant (20 million dollars) by Hozo-SHK, part of the Shantuo Agricultural Machinery group. The production intended for the European market goes through several development stages: tractors and components imported from China, paint line created and components produced on site to give the tractors a more pronounced local feel.

Case study 5
The setting up of Shanghai Maling in the Czech Republic as a supply base for Central European countries
One of the most interesting examples of the buoyancy of Chinese firms, and their desire for recognition in world markets, was given to us during an interview with the director of Shanghai Maling in the Czech Republic. The history of this firm is a true 'success story' that runs counter to hackneyed *clichés* and underlines the ability of Chinese firms for adaptation and initiative internationally.

Box 6   Shanghai Maling

Shanghai Maling is a subsidiary of the public group Guangming Food (also called Bright Food), specialising in the production of canned meat (mainly pork). Set up in the Czech Republic since 2007 its main outlets are in Central Europe, whilst the other foreign markets are supplied by Chinese factories of the parent company. Shanghai Maling currently has seventy employees, sixty of them local.

Its director states that he has tremendous freedom of action.

The Shanghai Maling's setting up in the Czech Republic, which was preceded by exports, has come about through a combination of two main factors: firstly, the presence in the Czech Republic and Central Europe of huge canned meat consumers and secondly, the Czech Republic's joining the European Union in 2004 which encouraged access to a vast market as well as enhanced health and food regulations, thereby helping to improve product quality. Other factors combined to realise the investment: first, an official visit by the Chinese Prime Minister, second, the firm being situated 100 km from Prague in an area where labour costs are 30 per cent to 50 per cent below Prague levels and which has a high rate of unemployment, make it eligible for public job creation aids.

The Shanghai Maling's expansion in the Czech Republic and neighbouring countries over the forthcoming years seems certain, whereas Western European countries are not involved for the moment given their distinctive culinary traditions. The firm has already expanded once and it intends to increase its annual production five times over to achieve 50,000 tonnes. The Maling brand has an excellent reputation in Czech Republic and in neighbouring countries, which is not common for a Chinese brand.

From the start the firm counted on the quality of its products (another surprising characteristic which runs counter to the usual *clichés*): the meat is imported from Western Europe (Spain and Belgium). The meat is 'second quality' according to the Western Europe standards, but its quality is nevertheless better than the so-called 'best quality' which is on sale in Central Europe. The cans are supplied by a French company established in the Czech Republic and the spices come from a local subsidiary of a Dutch firm. All components are European in origin except for the vitamin C which is added – China is now the only producer of vitamin C in the world – which precludes it being labelled 100 per cent 'made in Europe'. It is not without irony that the company director we interviewed showed us products copied by a Czech firm and a Romanian firm. Sold more cheaply for less quality, the cans

19 *GEO Magazine*, December 2009.

have the same size, the same colours, and even a brand designed to confuse with similar graphics with Chinese characters! The similarity is striking, as we observed.

The firm has good prospects. It is even considering to delocalise some of the Shanghai production activities to the Czech Republic. There are many reasons for this: ensure to Asian clients, mainly in Singapore, South Korea and South-East Asia, that the production is of good quality and meets the European standards which are reckoned to be drastic. The impact of transport costs from transferring the activity is not a problem as ships unloading in Hamburg frequently return to China empty. Besides, the cost of transporting an equivalent 20 foot container between China and Germany has dropped in 2010 from 1,400 dollars to less than 300 dollars, which has smashed the upwards trend of transports costs which until then seemed unavoidable.[19]

In conclusion, it seems that Shanghai Maling's in the Czech Republic has withstood the economic crisis relatively well. The firm has coped well with the global downturn in sales sparked by the crisis: the market has remained stable in the Czech Republic although sales have dropped in the neighbouring countries (Hungary and Romania especially).

3.4 The resilience of Chinese and Indian pre-crisis investments in Europe

It is not easy to monitor the acquisitions made by Chinese and Indian firms in Europe since 2000 in order to analyse the impact of the crisis. Indeed, if new investments are generally well covered by economic media, the same does not apply to plant closures or activity reduction through layoffs, unless they generate substantial social programmes. Therefore, without claiming exhaustiveness, several observations can be put forward and preliminary evidence can be drawn as follows.

First, the effects of the financial crisis are at least unequal across sectors and sub-sectors, and there is also variation according to European countries.

Second, Chinese firms have found that some of their buyouts have endured or prospered while others have closed down to fold back on the Chinese market, leading to delocalisation, or onto third world markets considered more profitable. Some failures may not be a direct result of the crisis but rather of problems or failures specific to the investors: poor accounting analysis, under-estimation of required financing, poor understanding of socio-cultural practices in the host country – e.g., difficult relations with trade unions and former directors, management weaknesses.

Third, the problems encountered by Indian investors already present in Europe are not restricted to the peripheral countries but include their core bases – the United Kingdom and Germany. One such example is the closure by Bharat Forge of its Scottish plant, Scottish Stamping, acquired in 2005, whilst the group's German plants, still profitable, were kept open. The automotive car parts manufacturer Amtek Auto is on the point of closing its plants abroad except for two UK sites. Mahindra Forging closed its Walsall Stokes plant in the United Kingdom in 2009 and delocalised the low-margin productions to India.

Four, the liquidation of the aluminium producer, Trevira, acquired in 2004 by the Indian Reliance Group, can also be mentioned. Consider also, for instance, the liquidation of the German and Swedish subsidiaries of Sakthi Sugar (one of the leading Indian sugar cane producers), the closure of the Austrian subsidiary of Vardhman Polytex (textile fibre producer) and the European disengagement of Wockhardt due to financial difficulties.

3.4.1   Good resistance to the crisis for some sectors

Overall, buyouts of European firms focused on a search for leading-edge technologies and brands have resisted, since the management and engineering teams have been retained and efforts have been made on both sides to overcome the cultural problems, which always requires some time. Simply remember the difficulties encountered by the European firms when they first invested in China. Note that links between some investors and the Chinese State, dreaded by some Western observers for strategic reasons, have proved in some cases to be protection coverage for the survival of acquired European firms, avoiding on the way redundancy programmes in sectors and regions already under stress (see case study 6) or reducing its impact (see case studies 9a and 9b).

Case study 6
The unquestionable success of BlueStar Silicones
BlueStar Silicones was created in 2007 by the China BlueStar group, a subsidiary of the public Chinese group ChemChina, following a buyout of the French company Rhodia Silicone. The firm has followed an external growth strategy in Europe between 2004 and 2007, which led to the acquisition of three European firms with recurring financial difficulties but indisputable know-how. The three firms were Adisseo (animal feed) and Rhodia Silicone (silicone) in France, and Fibres Worldwide (carbon fibres) in the United Kingdom. The Rhodia Silicone headquarters in Lyon were kept.

Box 7   BlueStar Silicones

The firm has two major production sites upstream of its activity, one at Saint-Fons (France) and the other at Xinghuo (China). It has nine other production sites in Germany, Italy, Spain, United States, Brazil and China. The main markets are Europe and China. Its 2008 turnover was 600 million Euros, including 400 in Europe. The company has a total workforce of three thousand employees, half of whom are based in China.

Blue Star Silicones Europe is run by a French national who was previously part of the Rhodia management team.

These three buyouts are nowadays considered successful

both for the Chinese and the European sides. The synergies have been totally effective: one side has increased its skills and boosted its positions (leading technologies, access to world safety and environmental standards, good quality, reliable products and management knowledge) and the other has seen its business saved and enhanced, including during the crisis.

The acquisition of Rhodia Silicone by China BlueStar, which until then had known how to produce silicone but lacked the upstream technologies and had no downstream presence, allowed it to diversify and increase its added value. It must be said that the China BlueStar directors knew the French firm well from the inside as they had enjoyed a partnership/sub-contracting relationship for several years. It was a sound firm but running out of steam; it nevertheless held fifth place worldwide in its sector. All the worldwide Rhodia production sites were kept, including in China, and all the necessary investments have been made to date. Unsurprisingly, the bought-out firm has expanded under the new name of BlueStar Silicones.

The new shareholders have elected to keep the management team and the executives and engineers on site; the activity of the European production units has also been maintained, with some reorganisation. This choice was partly dictated by the difficulty in finding high-class, English-speaking personnel in China with extensive international experience. Only three Chinese nationals work in the French subsidiary, whereas about thirty French nationals work on BlueStar Silicones' Chinese sites. The manager we met considers himself to have tremendous freedom despite being under the control of the Chinese headquarters.

The customers have not been put off by the new shareholders: they quickly realised that they could continue to place their trust in the firm, given the on-going quality of products marketed by the new company. The parent company has mainly had to face up to cultural problems when managing BlueStar Silicones in France, but they have been contained easily by retaining the management team.

A few differing viewpoints were expressed during our interview: the Chinese managers are more inclined to invest in hardware (building factories, purchasing equipment) than in software (human resources, technical skills, marketing expertise). They also place more emphasis on increasing turnover, unlike their counterparts who focus on improving the added value. Beyond the undeniable cultural differences, this also conveys a different development level in firms.

It is also important to remember that that Chinese State support for China BlueStar, and therefore its subsidiary BlueStar Silicones, has helped it through the crisis without damage and without a redundancy scheme, despite collapsing sales and income in 2009. The new Chinese management nevertheless found itself up against the North American investment fund Blackstone, holder of 20 per cent of the China BlueStar capital, which defended a short-term vision.

The final outcome is convincing. The European facilities have become highly efficient with productivity ten times higher than in the Chinese factories: the 140 employees at the French Saint-Fons factory produce almost as much as the 1,500 employees in the Chinese Xinghuo factory. But beyond this flattering observation, questions are being raised over the future of the company, notably in the light of cost price differences between Chinese and European plants, mainly for the basic activities. Transferring production to China ultimately seems inevitable due to sustainably lower production costs. This prospect is intensified by the high level of anti-dumping duties taken in Europe on products originating in China such as silicon, the firm's base material. China has substantial silicon reserves. Add to this that fixed costs are higher in France than in China.

Although the Chinese shareholders have so far played the game correctly to restructure the former Rhodia sites and improve their efficiency, it is obvious that they will not expand

20 The same 'copy and paste' operation also took place for the main Adisseo factory bought out by the same shareholder.

their capacities in the future as market prospects for the years to come are not in France or even Europe, but in China and other developing countries. The relative share of Europe in the group's turnover continues to decrease. This is the context for a new factory currently being built in China, a certified 'copy and paste' of the French Saint-Fons factory.[20] The current director of the French firm even intends to finish his career in China.

Case study 7
The on-going success stories of Chinese telecommunication equipment manufacturers

It is interesting to underline the success of Huawei Technologies and Zhong Xing Telecommunication Equipment Company (ZTE) in Europe despite the economic crisis. They have expanded their facilities and created new service units and research centres. In 2009, Huawei Technologies took the second place in the mobile network equipment market from Nokia Siemens, almost doubling its market share. The Swedish company Ericsson held on to first place.[21]

Huawei Technologies continues to generate numerous successes in Europe (see Box 8 below).

Both Chinese firms have continued to develop their European R&D centres in recent years, sometimes, ironically, on sites abandoned by their direct competitors (Nokia and Alcatel), due to an increasing proportion of their resources dedicated to R&D. In 2009, Huawei Technologies became the fourth largest firm worldwide for patent registrations.

---

21 According to the 2009 Market Research Report for the Global Wireless Communication Equipment, the world market shares of the global equipment providers was Ericsson, Huawei, Nokia and Siemens, ZTE, Alcatel Lucent with, respectively, market shares of 28.2 per cent, 22.1 per cent, 19 per cent, 12.6 per cent and 9.2 per cent (www.cn-c114.net/583/a499857.html).

> **Box 8** *Huawei Technologies continues its commercial breakthrough in Europe*
>
> Creation of very high-speed broadband optical connections between Paris, London and Amsterdam for the Netherlands operator KPN;
>
> Roll-out of 3G mobile networks in the Czech Republic for Telefonica;
>
> Construction of the Norwegian fourth-generation mobile network, to replace networks built by Ericsson and Nokia in a country which was for many years part of their game preserve;
>
> Signing contracts (12/2009) to supply two new base stations to SFR in two Southern French regions and to supply mobile phones to both stations.

Mr Paquet, Vice-President of Huawei France stated: *We are not followers, we are starting to innovate before the others.* Indeed, the group's fundamental research centre in Cergy-Pontoise (France), in operation since September 2009, and its Internet technologies demonstration centre in Darmstadt (Germany) stand out among its most striking set-ups in Europe; a new marketing and strategy research centre is also planned for Basingstoke (United Kingdom).

Huawei Technologies is starting to launch products under its own name in Europe: its USB 3G+ key (since end 2009) and telephones now bear its name.

The other Chinese telecommunication equipment manufacturer, ZTE, launched a new European development strategy in 2009, with France at its heart.

Although ZTE started its European market penetration campaign in the low-cost slot, nevertheless with a 'tailor-made' product range – basically PC network cards, mobile phones, USB 3G+ keys without brand for SFR and Orange – the firm now sells products under its own name and is seeking to position itself in more elaborate products. Europe is a direct target for this new strategy and the European operators in the sector are encouraging ZTE to take this route in order to share the costs of marketing and promoting offers.

The group is targeting the ultra low-cost mobile market and is looking to make touch-screen telephones more accessible as an alternative to the iPhone. It has therefore enlisted the help of South Korean consultancies to improve the design of its phones. Early in 2010, ZTE launched its first mobile on the market under its own colours (the X760) in partnership with Bouygues Télécom and a Google Android Phone. The plan is to launch a solar-powered Android and a Netbook under its own name also. In December 2009, ZTE enhanced its European setting-up by reorganising into large geographical divisions in which France occupies a central place. The headquarters of the division covering Western Europe, Eastern Europe and North America is located in Boulogne-Billancourt (France), thereby taking over from the division set up in 2004 for Western Europe only. This extension created 80 new jobs in addition to the 120 existing ones. The group is also very present in France; its market share doubled between 2008 and 2009 and now stands at 6 per cent.

Lastly, ZTE is entering into partnerships with the main European telephone operators, like the historical Spanish operator Telefonica to launch phones under the Movistar brand destined for South American markets.

3.4.2 Recovery after initial difficulties

Case study 8
The buyout of 'Conserves de Provence–Le Cabanon' by Xinjiang Chalkis
It is interesting to consider this pioneering buyout in 2004, with now a certain easing back, as the Chinese directors encountered many difficulties in the first years, with numerous cultural problems (and a legal settlement in 2008). The operation can these days be considered successful inasmuch as both parties have got something out of it. For the French side,

---

Box 9a *Conserves de Provence–Le Cabanon*

Conserves de Provence–Le Cabanon emanated from an agricultural cooperative created in 1947 in Camaret-sur-Aigues (France) by some one thousand tomato producers who wished to pool their resources in a tomato cannery (tomato *purée*, peeled tomatoes). The initial business was broadened to a range of sauces and cooked produces based on fresh vegetables (like *ratatouille*). In 1984, a subsidiary specialising in marketing the cooperative products was created: S. A. Le Cabanon.

The firm faced its first difficulties in 1998 with the elimination of customs' duties on primary processed products (tomato *purée* lost 50 per cent of its sales value) and increased competition, especially from Chinese producers with the advantage of particularly low labour costs. Their tomato *purée* has the advantage of inexpensive labour and arrives in Europe at a lower cost than local fresh tomatoes which, on top of everything, have to be processed. Profits dropped as a result and the firm started to lose money. It had to find a buyer if it was to survive.

At the same time, in 2005, one of its main suppliers of tomato purée, Chalkis, was looking to set up in France (heart of Europe, excellent gastronomic reputation). The matter was soon settled with a 50 per cent equity investment, increasing to 100 per cent in 2006 for an investment of about 15 million Euros.

---

the business and 141 jobs have been saved. For the Chinese side, the directors are satisfied to have had the chance to access know-how, a 'fine brand' and a logistics and sales platform. The result is a new dimension for their business: more elaborate products and new markets with extra added value. Contributions of this type are especially valuable for their

Box 9b   Xinjiang Chalkis, the buyer

Xinjiang Chalkis is a company specialised in tomato processing: tomato *purée* and ketchup. It is the leading Chinese group in its sector and the second worldwide behind the American firm Morningstar Farms, part of the Kellogg group.

The group was founded in 1994 in Urumqi as a national company with strong links to its province Xinjiang, via XPCC (Xinjiang Production and Construction Corp.), an economic development and semi-military body operating mainly in agriculture and food. It is run by Liu Yi, its founder and a former soldier.

Since the group's listing on the Shenzhen Stock Exchange in 2000, its capital has been split between XPCC (about 45%), its director and miscellaneous private shareholders.

The firm currently has 33 factories in China (Xianjin, Gansu, Inner Mongolia, Tianjin) and one in France. It produces about 300,000 tonnes of tomato-based products.

The firm has a global market as Chinese consumers still use very little tomato *purée* and sauces derived from it. The main customers are basically industrialists.

Chalkis now operates in France via its subsidiary Chalton based in Tianjin (1,400 employees in China).

The firm's turnover fluctuates between 500 and 800 million dollars depending on the year and the situation (tomato prices); the *Conserves de Provence–Le Cabanon* contribute by about 20 million.

The firm has sales offices in Moscow, Kiev and Alma Ata; it is also present in Africa, Europe and the United States. It has plans to set up in Germany and the United Kingdom, while a new commercial subsidiary, Delitomat, has just been opened in France to expand the group's European market.

expansion prospects in China and worldwide. Once again, it is clear that the indirect support of the Chinese state for this buyout and the bailout of the firm's activities proved crucial.

At the beginning, there was a French company running out of steam, forced to shut its doors and a Chinese investor with substantial financial resources, seeking to prop up its international expansion.

All things considered, the above example was successful, but this outcome was far from being easy at the start, given the huge problems, mainly cultural, faced by the Chalkis directors in the years following the acquisition:

- they were not accustomed to having their orders questioned and were very unsettled by the place held by the unions in France (which they deemed rather as agitators) and by the state of mind of employees;
- they were disorientated by the French accounting standards which differed from those they were accustomed to use in China under the international accounting standard for a group listed on the Stock Exchange;
- they had communication problems with consumers: Chinese products were not always well received and local tomato producers were extremely critical of them; they did not want to know that the majority of major French and European brands in the sector purchased their tomato *purée* in China (and French consumers did not know this).

To these difficulties were added falling sales (subsequently made worse by the crisis), delays in the deliveries to their customers (mainly supermarkets which are very demanding over delivery times) and various technical problems which delayed the introduction of new production lines.

It was inevitable that the firm faced a legal settlement in 2008, but a positive outcome was finally achieved by:

- injecting 2.3 million Euros into the company;

- paying off debts. The original feature was that the debts were paid in kind with the parent company granting 20,000 tonnes of tomato *purée* every year to *Conserves de Provence–Le Cabanon*;
- reducing the workforce from 300 to 141 people, all being French with the exception of four Chinese nationals (a director, an accountant, a purchasing manager and an interpreter);
- the arrival of a skilled manager, Michel Moragues (a former director of Conserves de France, hired timely) to run the firm, whose official function is operating director.

Finally, the directors of Chalkis were satisfied with their French acquisition that offered them new opportunities for the future:

- they acquired valuable know-how in the processing of tomato *purée*, which helped them go up in the product range;
- they acquired a brand and a label which they have not fully operated but which will allow them to build up their reputation in China and throughout the world. If we take the case of China, the tomato *purée* and ketchup market is still in its infancy because it is a consumption that is not part of the Chinese food culture, i.e. Chinese eat fresh produce. However, the new generations are changing their habits and tomato sauce products seem to have a promising future;
- they are now present throughout the tomato production chain, from its cultivation to the sales and marketing of tomato-based preparations for consumers. They therefore apply stringent quality control to their supplies: most tomatoes processed in the group's factories are grown in Xinjiang, which has a similar climate to Provence;[22]

22 Lavender and vines are also grown there.

- they are not under pressure concerning payment deadlines for their raw materials;
- and, above all, they have cleverly taken advantage of this buyout to create two processing units in Tianjin, with the identical activity to the French factory at Camaret-sur-Aigues but with far lower processing costs and cost prices, as they receive substantial aid from their home province (Xinjiang) and the central Chinese Government encouraging the 'Go West' Policy towards the rural provinces in the West of China.

In conclusion, the Chalkis directors currently believe they will not be overtaken in terms of quality-price ratio for many years.

3.4.3 Mixed results for other sectors

Case study 9
Chinese investments in the machinery and equipment sector
The Chinese positioning in this sector in Europe is mainly motivated by the quest for technical, often cutting-edge know-how, to improve the technical level of Chinese factories. The aim is sometimes to serve European markets.

Germany remains very attractive for Chinese investors. Actually, Chinese firms have made many acquisitions in Germany since the start of the millennium in the mechanical engineering sector (Hay, Milelli and Shi, 2008). They have continued with similar motivations and by seizing opportunities in the shape of German firms weakened by the current crisis.

One particularly interesting case is Sany Heavy (public

23 100 million Euros have been invested.
24 The key factors influencing our decision in favour of the Mühlenerft commercial zone were its proximity to Cologne, the excellent connections to the seaports, the sufficient supply of qualified staff, the professional and personal commitment in the town administrations of Bedburg and Bergheim and the outstanding service of the state agency NRW Invest.

works equipment)[23] choosing to set up a production and R&D centre in Cologne for its first venture into Europe. Its directors believe that it must favour to climb the value chain and facilitate access to the European market by better adaptation to the constraints and local standards and a reduction of transport costs (heavy goods).[24]

Another example was the buyout by the New Jack Sewing Machine Co. at the end of 2009 of two sewing machine companies, Bullmer and TopCut, with their assets being pooled into a single company.

Overall, based on interviews with the German Investment Promotion Agency, it seems that investments made at the start of the millennium in this sector in Germany have been quite successful and have resisted both the economic crisis and the ensuring recession well. Admittedly, certain difficulties have slackened the momentum to increase production capacities of bought-out firms, but the activities have been maintained. The Chinese investors see an advantage in producing in Germany, because they can benefit from well-qualified, expert local manpower, leading-edge technologies and specific know-how, all of which guarantee success. The brands acquired open the door to the world market: although the cost price and resulting selling price are higher than in China, the added value and margins generated are also higher. The Director of Beijing No.1 Machine Tool which bought out the German company Waldrich Coburg five years ago, is delighted with the acquisition: *The respect that German products enjoy throughout the world has been a decisive factor in our success. It guarantees that the added value we generate here is very high. I sell the same products in Germany for 100 Euros that I would sell in China for 50–60 Euros.*

It is also important to underline that German labour costs, among the highest in OECD countries, are not, ultimately, unacceptable for Chinese investors. This view is confirmed by

25 *Source:* Satisfied Chinese investors: Investment decisions rewarding, in *German Investment Magazine*, Vol. 1, April 2010.

the Chairman of the German subsidiary of Minmetals: *Many people believe that personnel costs in Germany are too high. However, when you calculate all the costs together, you realize that this is merely a preconception. Wages appear to be lower in southern Europe, but when you include all the various taxes in your calculation, you discover that the costs there are no lower there than they are here.*[25]

There are many similar examples, like the successful buyout of Zhafir Plastic in 2007, a company specialising in injection moulding machines, by Haitian Plastics, which has just expanded its factory at Ebermannsdorf (an extra 4,300 m^2) and acquired more efficient equipment to produce even more energy-saving machines for the world market. The directors of Haitian Plastics highlight the technological springboard and the innovative environment open to them in Germany, which allow them to satisfy the most demanding consumers. The firm continues to produce bottom-end products in China as an extension to its range.

Not everything is perfect, however, and some Chinese investments in the equipment sector have run into trouble, with orders falling because of the crisis. The result has been employee redundancies and even production site closures with, depending on circumstances, simply keeping sales offices open and/or delocalising production to China.

Not all the failures and problems encountered by the Chinese firms are known, and we discovered during our surveys that an investment listed previously in the buyouts no longer existed as we sought to meet the directors.

In addition, the listed failures are those perceived as such by the Europeans, which does not however mean that Chinese firms agree with this view when considering the acquisition of technical and managerial know-how and famous brands. They prefer to talk of mixed success.

Examples in Germany and France illustrate this aspect:

26 For the record, another Chinese group, Avic, was also seeking to acquire the firm at the same period.

In Germany, the closure of E-Mill (construction tools), bought out by Bosai Minerals in 2007.

In France, firstly the filing for compulsory liquidation in 2009 of Two Cast (manufacturer of moulds for Michelin tyres and motor parts), with three manufacturing sites (Saint-Satur, Villefontaine and Saint-Eloy). The firm had been bought out in June 2008 by Hebei Hongye Machinery for 10,000 Euros.[26] The company could not, however, withstand foreign competition and went down suddenly at the end of 2008 with the crisis. It is also possible that some customers were destabilised and distrustful of a Chinese takeover. The firm was sold to Fonderies Lory (France) in January 2010.

Then came the problems encountered by Goss International (rotary presses with production sites at Montataire and Nantes) in a joint venture since 2008 with Shanghai Electric Group alongside the North American pension fund Matlin Patterson. The groups' workforce was cut drastically in 2009 and the Nantes site escaped closure by a whisker. The future of the company is still in jeopardy.

Lastly, the employee cuts in the firm Gate France (Saint-Rémy-de-Maurienne), part of the Johnson Electric group, specialising in the manufacture of small engines for car manufacturing.

Case study 10
The falling back of the Indian IT service sector in Europe
As stated previously (par. 3.2.4), although software and associated services remain in the lead in Europe, its relative weight has changed. There are two possible causes which are not related: firstly, the effect of the financial crisis which unquestionably slowed down demand for this type of service, especially in continental Europe where outsourcing is still in

27 2009–2010, Tata Consultancy Services, activity report.

its infancy. For example, in 2009, this geographical area (excluding the United Kingdom) only accounted for 10 per cent of the total turnover of the IT subsidiary of Tata Consultancy Services (TCS). Secondly, there was a pause in the number of new investments, which is quite common after such a sustained investment phase by Indian IT firms in Europe since 2000. Note that TCS was a pioneer for Indian investment in Europe. It is true, that since opening its first office in the United Kingdom in 1975, TCS has opened 22 offices in twelve European countries. Therefore, Europe is the first foreign base for TCS based on sites number, thereby outstripping North America, despite the fact that the latter is still holding the lion's share of its consolidated turnover, with a market share of 52 per cent in 2009.[27] At the beginning of the 2000s, it was followed in Europe by its counterparts and competitors, Wipro Technologies and Infosys, with 21 per cent and 25 per cent respectively of their 2009 consolidated turnover represented by Europe, and which are now struggling to increase this market share, especially in continental Europe.

Chapter 4

Outcomes and Prospects

As expected, the global financial crisis had several effects on Chinese and Indian investments in Europe. Our main findings can be summarized as follows.

The question is: would the effects be simply provisional or more durable and conducive to significant change?

Chinese and Indian investments are now part of the world investment landscape: they are helping to swing wealth and economic power towards 'Southern countries'. Indeed, developing countries in general, and emerging economies in particular, have been growing appreciably faster than developed economies over the past decade.

Europe is still attractive to them despite their keen interest in countries or areas with natural resources.

The three largest countries by market size (United Kingdom, Germany and France) remain the main recipients of Chinese and Indian investments in Europe, even if the United Kingdom is improving its attractiveness whereas Central Europe seems to have suffered more from the crisis.

Chinese and Indian investments are showing commitment levels which are on average lower than before the crisis.

Paradoxically, mergers and acquisitions have been less affected by the crisis than greenfield investments, both for opportunity and strategic reasons. Indeed, this mode of entry allows new investors to keep pace with their 'catch-up' strategies in a context of unabated globalisation (Mathews 2006).

Indian investors have been affected far more than Chinese

investors in Europe. Two explanations can be put forward: for China, firm support from central government and local governments nurturing 'local champions', and a larger range of involved sectors (or sub-sectors), and in some cases with positions bolstered by the crisis. Conversely, Indian investments remain positioned in sectors (IT services, car manufacture and pharmaceuticals) more affected by the downturn in demand in Europe. Besides, they are basically private firms with more limited access to financial resources, even for large diversified groups.

Rising Chinese and Indian investments in the European automotive sector – from car parts manufacturers to assemblers – with numerous M&As. It mirrors the buoyant domestic market for cars in both countries, with China outstripping the United States in 2009 as the first market worldwide.

Chinese investments made overseas somehow reflect the new potential growth of the Chinese domestic market for the future. As a result, numerous firms are climbing the value chain by combining in house development and acquisition/ absorption of foreign know-how, particularly in Developed countries (Zeng and Williamson, 2007).

Access to the European markets has been partly supplanted since the crisis by the desire of Chinese and Indian firms to assert their positions in their home country, to gain a march on their domestic competitors or to catch up with foreign subsidiaries, especially in China (Gaulier *et al.*, 2010). They therefore seek to acquire specific assets in Europe, to convert them into firm specific advantages to reduce their competiviveness gap with established multinational firms. They include upstream strengths such as technological superiority,

28 See: State-Owned Enterprises (SOEs) increase overseas investment, *China Daily*, 18/09/2009.
29 These firms are under direct control of the State-owned Assets Supervision and Administration Commission. By the end of the year, the centrally-administered SOEs extended their businesses into 127 countries by setting up or investing in 1,791 companies worldwide, (MOFCOM).

and downstream strengths such as brand recognition and marketing skills.

Chinese firms tend to increase the proportion of their activity dedicated to production compared with Indian investments.

The place and role of public actors in the internationalisation process of Chinese firms is striking, and makes Chinese multinationals stand out clearly from the position of Indian investors. According to the Chinese Ministry of Commerce (MOFCOM):[28] *the centrally-administrated State firms[29] contributed 64 per cent of China's overseas direct investment in value in 2008. Eighty-six per cent, or 117 out of the 136 centrally-administrated State-Owned Enterprises invested a total of 35.74 billion dollars last year, with the overall ODI amounting to 55.91 billion dollars in 2008.* This means that Chinese firms can take advantage of conditions of access to financial resources which their Indian competitors and industrial countries do not have, especially during the crisis.

Interestingly, Chinese public support for its firms during times of crises provides a form of liquidity insurance. They can help European firms like BlueStar Silicones in France to overcome the crisis, and also have a welfare effect by avoiding layoffs.

By and large, Chinese and Indian experience confirms that firm specific advantages are not absolute or universal, but contingent upon home country factors in particular, as strikingly illustrated by Chinese companies when they venture abroad. It challenges the convergence view on a 'Western model' and confirms the assumption of scholars such as Kerr (1983) with a convergence on a first tier – e.g. plant layout, accounting method – while there is no convergence so far on a second tier consisting of values, beliefs and behaviours.

Lastly, let's acknowledge the importance of bilateral diplomatic relations in stimulating investment flows, especially for

30 Quoted by Ding Qingfen, *China Daily*, 27/04/2010.
31 Whereas 30 per cent have no intention of doing so.

China as it is still, for a large part, a State-led capitalism, especially if one takes into consideration the array of outward investment flows (table 2).

In conclusion, we will draw some prospects for the European economies resulting from the presence and/or arrival of Chinese and Indian investors.

Chinese and Indian investments in Europe are unquestionably bound to continue as they are an integral part of their international engagement. For the former, mention can be made of forecasts by the China Council for the Promotion of International Trade,[30] taken from a survey of the intentions of Chinese firms to invest abroad: 26 per cent of firms surveyed intend to invest in the next twelve months[31] and 61 per cent in the next two to five years. Nonetheless, the international path is still a bumpy road for Chinese enterprises. It reminds us of the validity of the 'psychic distance' concept (and the 'liability of foreignness'), and the need for them to overcome the uncertainty relative to the difference in several cultural aspects, along with business practices and regulations (Johanson and Wiedersheim-Paul, 1975; Hofstede, 1980). Actually, Chinese firms, with their relative lack of expertise and experience in the internationalisation field, are still in a learning process. Reckless or even predatory strategies are not excluded from particular enterprise but this risk would be controlled.

Chinese public authorities who proposed a financial help in late 2010 to some distressed European countries were basically motivated by political reasons, with the desire not to stir nationalistic reactions and resulting protectionism, and to avoid the rise of anti-Chinese feelings even if Europeans in general don't see Chinese investments in Europe as a Trojan horse.

Lastly, India and the European Union have just started negotiating a free trade agreement which includes a direct investment section. Its ratification should stimulate the bilateral flows by offering guarantees to investors on both sides.

References

Altenburg T., Schmitz H. and Stamm A. (2008), Breakthrough? China and India's transition from production to innovation, *World Development*, Vol. 36 (2): 325–44.

Athere S. and Kapur S. (2009), The internationalization of Chinese and Indian firms – Trends, motivations and strategy, *Industrial and Corporate Change*, Vol. 18 (2): 209–21.

Cogman D. and Tan J. (2010), A lighter touch for post merger integration, *McKinsey Quarterly*, January.

Cui L. and Jiang F. (2009), FDI entry mode of Chinese firms: a strategic behaviour, *Journal of World Business*, Vol. 44 (4): 434–44.

Dunning John H. (1981), Explaining the international direct investment position of countries: Toward a dynamic and development approach, *Weltwirtschaftliches Archiv*, Vol. 117: 30–64.

Gaulier G., Jarreau J., Lemoine F., Bonnet S. and Unal D. (2010), Chine : la fin du modèle de croissance extravertie, *La Lettre du CEPII*, No. 298.

Hay F. and Milelli C. (2009), Un nouveau regard sur les délocalisations des entreprises françaises en Chine, *Accomex*, Vol. 89: 55–60.

Hay F., Milelli C. and Shi Y. (2008), Présence et stratégies des firmes chinoises et indiennes en Europe : une perspective dynamique et comparative, Rapport d'étude pour le compte de la Direction Générale des Entreprises, Ministère de l'Économie, des Finances et de l'Emploi, Paris.

Hofstede G. (1980), *Culture's Consequences: International differences in work-related values*, Beverly Hills: Sage Publications.

Ilan A., Chang J., Fetscherin M., Latemann C. and McIntyre J. (2009), Globalization with Chinese characteristics, *Chinese Management Studies*, Vol. 3 (1): 8–10.

Johanson J. and Wiedersheim-Paul F. (1975), The internationalization of the firm: Four Swedish cases, *Journal of Management Studies*, Vol. 12: 305–22.

References

Kerr C. (1983), *The Future of Industrial Societies: Convergence or continuing diversity*, Cambridge, MA: Harvard University Press.

Mathews S. A. (2006), Dragon multinationals: New players in the 21st century globalization, *Asia Pacific Journal of Management*, Vol. 23, 93–113.

Milelli C., Hay F. and Shi Y. (2010), Chinese and Indian Firms in Europe: Characteristics, impacts and policy implications, *International Journal of Emerging Markets*, Vol. 5 (3–4): 377–97.

Morck R., Yeung B. and Zhao M. (2008), Perspectives on China's outward foreign direct investment, *Journal of International Business Studies*, Vol. 39 (3): 337–50.

Nolan P. (2001), *China and the Global Economy: National champions, industrial policy and the big business revolution*, New York: Palgrave.

Pradhan J. (2009), *The global economic crisis: Impact on Indian outward investment* (http://ssrn.com/abstract=1515678).

Pradhan J. and Singh N. (2008), *Outward FDI & knowledge flows: A study of the Indian automotive sector*, WP 2008–10, ISID, New Delhi.

Tang F., Gao X. and Li Q. (2008), Knowledge acquisition and learning strategies in globalization of China's enterprises, in I. Alon and J. R. McIntyre(eds.), *Globalizing of Chinese enterprises*, New York: Palgrave.

Yeung H. W. and Liu W. (2008), Globalizing China: The rise of mainland Chinese firms in the global economy, *Eurasian Geography and Economics*, Vol. 49 (1): 57–86.

Yiu D. W, Lau C. M. and Bruton G. D. (2007), International venturing by emerging economy firms: The effects of firm capabilities, home country networks, and corporate entrepreneurship, *Journal of Business Studies*, Vol. 38 (4): 519–40.

Yusuf S., Nabeshima K. and Perkins D. H. (2007), China and India reshape global industrial geography, in: Winters A. & Yusuf S. (eds), *Dancing with the Giants – China, India and the global economy*, The World Bank and the Institute of Policy Studies, Singapore.

Zeng M. and Williamson P. J. (2007), *Dragons at our Door: How Chinese cost innovation is disrupting global competition*, Cambridge, MA: Harvard Business School Press.

Index

89

Index

G
Germany 14, 16, 18, 29, 32, 35, 36, 38, 39, 43, 45, 56, 60, 61, 62, 63, 67, 68, 72, 78, 79, 80, 81, 83
greenfield investments 8, 10, 14, 18, 22, 24, 30, 31, 45, 83

H
headquarters 22, 35, 47, 48, 49, 60, 66, 68, 69, 73
Huawei Technologies 35, 71, 72
Hungary 42, 48, 62, 63, 66

I
IT services 19, 27, 31, 45, 48, 84
international investment position 3, 7, 8, 10
Italy 14, 16, 18, 32, 33, 35, 38, 43, 52, 53, 61, 62, 68

J
Jaguar 20, 43
joint venture 23, 29, 31, 49, 52, 59, 81

L
labour costs 51, 62, 65, 74, 79
Land Rover 20, 43
Li & Fung Group 37, 53, 54
luxury (car, goods, sector, etc.) 37, 42, 52, 53, 56

M
marketing 2, 70, 72, 73, 74, 77, 85
mergers-and-acquisitions (M&As) 8, 10, 11, 12, 13, 14, 15, 16, 17, 18, 19, 20, 22, 30, 31, 84

N
Netherlands 14, 32, 33, 38, 43, 49, 72

Neusoft 35, 46, 47, 48
niche markets 20, 46

O
outsourcing 46, 54, 55, 81

P
partnership 50, 59, 69, 73
pharmaceuticals 19, 20, 36, 39, 84
photovoltaic 58, 59, 60
Poland 34, 63
portfolio investments 6, 8, 9, 44

R
R&D 22, 35, 48, 50, 60, 71, 79
Reliance Group 20, 67
renewable energies 26, 57, 58, 61
Romania 34, 60, 62, 63, 64, 66

S
Shanghai Maling 64, 65, 66
software 14, 16, 19, 20, 35, 36, 39, 40, 45, 46, 48, 49, 50, 70, 81
solar (farm, panel, plant) 26, 58, 60, 61, 73
South America 1, 14, 18
Spain 10, 32, 35, 60, 65, 68
specific assets 2, 26, 84
State-Owned Enterprises (SOEs) 15, 85
sub-contracting 46, 50, 53, 69
Suntech Power 16, 36, 60
Switzerland 47, 48, 52, 60, 62

T
takeover 16, 41, 81
Tata 20, 23, 43, 82
technology (technologies) 14, 23 26 28, 29, 35, 41, 46, 67, 69, 72, 79
telecommunications (equipment, sector) 2, 19, 35, 36, 39, 71–2